WALL STREET

Its Mysteries Revealed: Its Secrets Exposed

TOGETHER WITH *A Complete Course of Instruction in Speculation and Investment* AND *Rules for Safe Guidance Therein*

BY WILLIAM C. MOORE

FRASER PUBLISHING COMPANY

First Published 1921
by William C. Moore
New York

Fraser Publishing Company Edition

Box 494
Burlington, VT 05402

2nd printing 1988

ISBN: 0-87034-041-7
Library of Congress Catalog Card Number: 66-19018

Printed in the U.S.A.

CONTENTS

INTRODUCTION.

Many years of association with the speculatively inclined public both in a personal way and through correspondence has impressed me of the public need for a more general and intimate knowledge of speculation in stocks and commodities.

I believe that a work such as I have prepared will furnish the reader with the information and instruction most needful to guide him knowingly in market operations.

Only a very small percentage of those who trade in stocks and commodities have a general knowledge of speculative operations. Few persons who buy stocks, bonds, grain or cotton, understand the modus operandi involved in such transactions. The object of this book is to instruct the reader in every essential phase of speculation and investment and to guard him against the pit-falls of Wall Street; to set forth suggestions and practical general advice and instruction calculated to help and benefit the reader and to supply him with Rules necessary for his proper guidance in making market commitments.

If I shall have succeeded through the instrumentality of this work in helping my fellow men to avoid losses and to make profits in their speculative and investment ventures, I shall feel that I have performed a needed public service.

W. C. Moore.

New York, 1921.

I

SPECULATION AND THE SUBSIDIZED PRESS

It is not the purpose of this book to encourage speculation, but rather to assist those speculatively inclined to act knowingly and rightly. In short, to bring them to a realization of the fact that speculation is not a haphazard game of chance. Unfortunately however for themselves, most speculators act on the assumption that speculative commitments may be made on "news," impulse, opinion, judgment, "information," etc., and that these will bring desired results. Operations in the markets predicated on this false theory bring failures in Wall Street, on the Chicago Board of Trade and on the Cotton Exchange. Opinion, impulse, rumor, information and news are deceptive, misleading and treacherous guides in market operations. Those who base their market commitments on these "quick sands" are almost sure to lose through speculation. They may be successful temporarily, but in the end they will lose their capital. The reason for this natural, final outcome is this: They do not act in harmony with the laws of market movements. As a matter of fact, very few speculators know there are such laws, and 99% of speculators seem to prefer to disbelieve there are such laws. Every man who is well versed and is mentally balanced recognizes the fact that everything tangible and intangible is governed by natural laws. Every thought —every action—every movement—every cause and every effect is the logical result of natural laws. These laws are immutable and work out logically in spite of what we may believe or disbelieve or fail to understand. We must recognize these laws and we must act in harmony with them if we would have them bring their rewards marketwise. When these laws are violated they exact a penalty which is usually financial failure. To be successful in speculation we must recognize the fact that speculation is a scientific game and to attain success therein we must act in harmony with the laws that govern market movements.

The Subsidized Press

One should never lose sight of the fact that while speculation in stocks and commodities is a scientific game, it is played with "marked cards" and for the purpose of separating the "outsider" from his capital. The unsophisticated and unskilled trader or investor has only the shadow of a chance to come off victor in this speculative contest. Why? Because he acts on mental suggestion. He may imagine he is acting on judgment when he makes a commitment. His so-called judgment is formed from what he has read or heard. He has perhaps read an article or a paragraph in a newspaper, periodical, circular, booklet or letter extolling the merits of some particular stock. He does not stop to surmise the motive that prompted the publication of such laudatory comments. He does not take time to reason that the writer could not afford to give his services gratis, nor the publisher of such matter the space in his paper, periodical or other agency without a *quid pro quo.* He does not stop to ask himself if he is justified in assuming that in every instance where complimentary reference to any stock is made in print, it is paid for at the highest advertising rates. As I write this paragraph, I pick up an evening newspaper issued to-day. I turn to the financial section and read some of the laudatory paragraphs relating to listed stocks. The first paragraph that meets my eye says: "In quarters which ought to know the nature of these negotiations, it is believed Sumatra's earnings will be greatly increased, and on this theory insiders are predicting a better market for the shares." During the following 30 days, Sumatra advanced about 5 points, then declined 20 points during the following 30 days. Here's another from the same paper of the same date: "Those who should know what the market sponsors for Pan-American Pete. are doing say that a much higher selling level should be seen eventually," etc. Pan-American advanced about 5 points in the 30 days following, then slumped about 33 points. Still another in same issue of this paper: "In some quarters it is predicted that when U. S. Steel directors meet July 27 (1920), an extra will be declared," etc. Steel advanced about 2 points in the 30 days following, then declined 20 points in 60 days. Middle States Oil: "A good outside demand is noted for the stock. A belief that important developments are impending through the newly organized Imperial Oil Co.," etc. M. S. O. was then selling at about 29. Within 60 days it declined to 10¼. A drastic slump in all the high-priced Industrials, Oils, Rubbers, Motors, Steels, Sugars, Foods, etc., occurred in November and December following. Glance at the financial section of almost any influential New York newspaper or financial periodical on any day of the week and you are likely to read something quite as misleading as that above quoted.

The foregoing are only a few of the "good things" prepared daily for public consumption. In every issue of certain newspapers, and in other sheets and periodicals, the reader will find stuff similar in tenor to that quoted above. Of course, it is obvious to any thinking person that these favorable comments relating to particular stocks are suggestions to the public to buy such stocks. The venal press does not extol or compliment a stock, corporation or company gratuitously. "Reading ads." such as these bring a generous financial compensation to the press, but they are usually costly to the readers who act in accordance with their suggestions. Reading ads. are the most deceptive of all ads. so command the highest rates. When you see such ads. relating to stocks or other things, ask yourself, " what is the motive that suggested such reading matter?"

In special cases where the pools are manipulating the stocks so highly recommended by the financial paragraphers, the paragraphers or publishers share in the profits of the pools. The amount of profits made by the pools depends on their adroitness in manipulating the stocks or commodities. If they are being manipulated upward, then their profits will be in proportion to their success in "boosting" such stocks or commodities. Most of the leading newspapers in New York co-operate with the pools to "land" the public with stocks at the highest prices obtainable. These are what are called the subsidized or venal press.

The subsidized press is a part of the machinery of the Stock Exchange. It acts in harmony with the wishes and dictates of the Exchange. It shares in the profits of the so-called Inside Interests. The financial policy of the subsidized press is shaped by the Exchange. It must promote the interests of the Exchange or be penalized. The financial editors of the subsidized press are told how to shape the tenor of their market comments. These are usually bullish in tone when the Insiders have stocks for sale. The higher the prices, the more bullish are the suggestions of these docile financial writers. They execute the orders given them by the managers of the papers or periodicals, and they in turn receive *their* orders from those in control of the Exchange. If the market happens to be "dead" at the bottom after a general cleaning out of marginal accounts, and the Inside Interests desire to accumulate lines of long stocks at advantageous prices, then the tenor of the suggestions of the financial commentators and the little financial paragraphers is likely to be doleful or pessimistic.

This attitude of the subsidized sheets serves to cause further liquidation on the part of the public and to discourage buying by the outsiders.

Whatever attitude is assumed by this paid agency is always in the interest of the Insiders and against the interest of the outside public. The policy of such a press is to serve the Inside Interests—to help them remove the fleeces from the "lambs" which this same agency lures into the shearing place. The innocent, credulous and unsophisticated reader of such luring suggestions, if he acts in harmony with them, will add another fleece to the holdings of the Insiders. Without the subsidized press to help lure victims into the fleecing place, the Stock Exchange would not be the profitable institution it is.

The owners and managers of subsidized agencies are usually avaricious and covetous fellows. They are not averse to getting money by devious methods. They will submit to outside domination as to the policy of their paper or periodical if it promises a satisfactory financial return. The powers connected with the Stock Exchange are cognizant of this weakness and take advantage of it to promote their own financial interests. As an illustration of what the Stock Exchange does in relation to the subsidized press: It has a service man—"Friday"—who is located near the Exchange. The duties of this fellow is to censor financial advertisements. If any of these appear in the venal press which may tend to injure the Inside Interests or thwart their plans or purposes, the managers are "requested" through "Friday" to discontinue such advertisements, or be penalized. I have in mind the case of a leading and influential newspaper that 10 years ago had upwards of 250,000 circulation. The management was notified, so I was then told at the publication office, that the Stock Exchange had "requested" certain advertisements be discontinued and that the loss incident to such discontinuance would be made up through a sufficient amount of other financial advertising. From the day the "request" was complied with, that paper began to decline and was eventually sold as "junk" to a Sun worshipper.

For some years last past, I did and still do some advertising in other than the subsidized newspapers. In March, 1920, soon after the U. S. Supreme Court handed down its decision holding that stock dividends were not taxable, all of the profiteering corporation stocks were boosted to ridiculously high prices. The directors of these corporations, when they thought the stocks about as high as they could be safely manipulated, declared stock dividends; but before many of them had so declared these dividends, I inserted advertisements in certain newspapers advising the public against buying these manipulated profiteering stocks, or accepting profiteering stock dividends. That settled me so far as certain of these papers were concerned. They had, I presume, been "requested" by the Stock Exchange man "Friday" to refuse me further advertising space in those newspapers. You see I had hurt the Insiders in a financial way. In short, I had interfered with the game and prevented the Insiders from fleecing *all* of the lambs that would naturally have gravitated to the fleecing place. It is the policy of the Stock Exchange to allow no person or interest to interfere with the plans of the Insiders to "hook" the public. Truth made public is especially abhorrent to these Interests, so the venal press is muzzled and TRUTH suppressed. The subsidized organs are always ready and anxious to serve the interests that offer the best bribes. Such a press has little regard for ethics. It sells its influence to the highest bidder and there is no more fertile market than Wall Street affords. That is where it gets its biggest revenue for space in its columns. I know of the case of a man who a couple of years ago was working on a financial sheet at a moderate salary. During the period of the speculative orgy in 1919-20 he managed to accumulate upwards of half a million dollars. He knew practically nothing of the art of scientific speculation. The presumption is he was close to the manager of the subsidized paper that helped to promote the interests of certain Insiders at the expense of the dear public.

I know of a case where a steel magnate bought a large line of a certain stock at about 80. When it advanced to 111, he began to unload. Incidentally a certain subsidized New York evening paper was bulling it every day, predicting much "higher prices," etc. When the steel man had unloaded, this paper ceased calling attention of its readers to the "good thing." The stock a little later on declined into the 60's. Of course, it is taken for granted the manager of the paper received a liberal compensation for his influence in helping the steel profiteer to unload on the unsuspecting public. I have known of this profiteer advising some of his intimate friends to sell stocks short early in 1920 while he was preaching prosperity to the unsophisticated inhabitants throughout the steel and mining sections of Pennsylvania and West Virginia.

Scan the financial pages of any or all of the subsidized newspapers and periodicals published in New York and you will observe that they act in harmony. They are always commending named stocks to their readers. The less of intrinsic value such stocks possess, the stronger they are bulled. The nearer stocks reach their tops, the greater the efforts of the subsidized press to bull the market and to entice the outside public to buy. If the market gives an indication of a collapse or a reaction, the subservient press, in order to allay uneasiness or apprehension on the part of the credulous public, assures it that "it's only a natural, temporary set-back on technical adjustment." If the reaction extends further, then "the bears were busy trying to depress prices to-day, but they are getting themselves into a trap. The public should take advantage of these temporary recessions to buy stocks," etc., etc., ad nauseam. Day after day, this same misleading stuff appears in the financial sections of the subsidized press. It is there to help the Insiders who pay for such inspired suggestions. It is there for the purpose of misleading the outside public. It is there to influence the credulous outsiders to do what the Insiders desire them to do. It is there to cause the unwary outsiders to contribute (through their losses) to the profits of the Insiders; so whenever the innocent reader consults the financial section of the subsidized press for guidance in making his speculation or investment commitments, he puts himself in a class with lambs who go to wolves for advice.

It is quite possible, yea even probable, that the subsidized press may not relish the uncomplimentary charges I make against it. Still, I must not omit some of the undesirable features of the Wall Street game just because the exposure may hurt the feelings of the wolves who mask in sheep's clothing in order to deceive the lambs. The reader of these pages will not be likely to see any complimentary announcement, or any advertisement referring to this book in any subsidized newspaper or periodical—for obvious reasons. So, if you read in any newspaper or periodical uncomplimentary references to this book or to its author, that *per se* is proof that such paper or periodical is venal and one of the class referred to in the foregoing indictment.

II
STOCK EXCHANGE

Curb Market
Curb Stocks
Listed Stocks
Stock Brokers—Stock Manipulation

A Stock Exchange is an institution where purchases and sales of stocks and of bonds of Governments, Municipalities and Corporations may be made in accordance with the rules and regulations formulated by the Exchange.

The prehensory tentacles of the Stock Exchange reach out in every direction that promises financial profit. One of them reaches into the vaults of the banks; another stretches out and over into the National Capital; another holds in its prehensile grip, the venal press; another reaches deep into the pockets of the unsophisticated public; another is stretched out in a menacing way toward those who oppose or antagonize the Exchange. The bank that fails to accede to the demands of the Exchange, stands little chance to share in the extra profits of national, municipal and corporate loans. The influential politicians in Washington are generally anxious to be "touched" by the tentacles that reach over into the Capital. The purchaseable press is a willing hireling of the Exchange, so it deceives the public in order to serve its master. The Exchange employs every known method to bring "grist to the mill." It takes a toll from every source of supply. There is reason to believe that over 75% of all the money contributed by the public for speculative ventures never returns, but is absorbed by the inside members of the Stock Exchange and by other interests co-operating with them. Thus we see what useful members these Stock Exchange tentacles are for the Exchange, but at what a cost to the dear public.

Curb Market

This is an outside or street market where many stocks and a few bonds not listed on regular Stock Exchanges, are bought and sold. Most of the stocks dealt in on this market are low-priced issues selling at from a cent to a dollar and upwards a share. In New York, Curb trading devotes itself exclusively to those issues which have not yet been admitted to the list of a stock Exchange. Some of these shares have some intrinsic value while others are of unknown value. There is little or no data on which to base an estimate of the value or lack of value of the stocks dealt in on the Curb. Most of them are speculative to a high degree and rather hazardous to trade in, and for this reason I have never advised the purchase of Curb stocks.

Curb Stocks

Usually before a stock appears or is regularly quoted on the Broad Street Curb it is passed upon by the Curb Association and approved, but this has not been so in all cases. I know of swindling stocks that have been dealt in on the Curb and their prices quoted in reputable newspapers. Curb issues are popular with the uninitiated and credulous public—First, because they are low-priced; second, their initial appearance is accompanied by misleading bombastic advertisement in the newspapers. These are usually supplemented by circulars or prospectuses calculated to allure the unwary into buying them.

A large percentage of the so-called Curb stocks have little genuine value. This is especially so in the case of the very low-priced issues, many of which are questionable and some are practically worthless. The laxness in enforcing the laws relating to organizing and incorporating companies makes it easy for questionable characters to form and organize such combinations and to exploit the shares among the unwary. The usual plan for selling questionable issues to the public is: First, have the stocks listed or quoted on the Curb; second, have inserted in newspapers bombastic display advertisements of a luring character, usually misleading and misrepresenting in statement; third, sending out through the mails, circulars or prospectuses of a like tenor as the advertisements in the newspapers. These are addressed to credulous "prospects," the names being obtained from what are known as "sucker lists," i. e., the names of persons who have already been victims of some other questionable or swindling scheme. These names after being "worked" by one or more concerns, are in turn sold to other schemers. A "sucker list" is considered quite essential for the distribution of "fake" or worthless stocks.

These sucker lists are bought and sold at so much per 1,000 names. Every person who has bought questionable or worthless stocks, or who has written to the promoters thereof, or to the brokers handling such stuff, is considered a "sucker" and is so listed. You sometimes hear persons who have received a circular letter from a broker or exploiter observe: "I wonder how he got my name? I never wrote to that person!" Perhaps not, but he wrote to some other broker or exploiter of the same ilk and his name was sold, or exchanged for the name of some other sucker.

If the so-called sucker writes to the concern about the stocks, thus showing an interest, he is bombarded with urgent appeals to send in his order at once accompanied by check or cash. If he fails to respond within a reasonable time, an agent of the exploiters is sent to personaly importune the prospective victim.

Now if these prospective victims were to use their brains and do a little reasoning, they might save themselves from an almost certain loss. They might interrogate themselves something like this: If these shares I am offered are valuable and are likely to become more valuable or advance in price, as represented by the promoters or brokers, why don't they hold on to them? Why spend thousands of dollars in exploiting them? The gullible people who hand over their good money for such stocks are legion. Victims are drafted from all classes. The chances of much for little seem to lure them. It seems almost incredible that persons in good circumstances and apparently intelligent should be such easy victims of swindlers and schemers. If some of these victims were questioned about their purchases of low-priced stocks and surprise expressed that they were so indiscreet and lacking in good judgment, their reply would probably be something like this: "Oh! I bought them for a quick turn. I'll sell them when they show a good profit." That is to say, they hope and expect to sell to other "suckers" at a price above what they—the actual suckers—paid for the stocks. In 99 cases of 100, the fellow who bought expecting to unload on the fellow more credulous than himself, finds that he himself is the victim instead of the other fellow from whom he hoped to make a profit. Making profits off low-priced stocks bought on the curb, is about as probable as finding diamonds in the gutters. I have yet to find a person (brokers excepted) who made money and retained it by buying low-priced stocks on the Curb. I advise the reader of these lines to abstain from patronizing brokers or exploiters who specialize in such questionable or worthless issues.

There are many questionable stock issuing concerns who employ agents to peddle their issues. These fellows call on unsophisticated and unsuspecting persons—school teachers, widows, milliners, farmers, and others unfamiliar with stock schemes.

Not all Curb stocks may be classed with the "57 varieties" described in the preceding lines. Some stocks, like Standard Oil issues, are meritorious. The principal reason for keeping them on the Curb is that the S. O. Corporations do not want the outsiders to have any definite knowledge relating to their assets. This would be made public if the S. O. Subsidiaries were listed on the N. Y. Stock Exchange. There are some other stocks having merit that receive their initiation on the Curb and in the course of time are promoted to the Big Board (N. Y. Stock Exchange).

The number of Curb stocks that eventually find themselves in respectable company is quite limited. Mostly all Curb stocks continue to remain Curb issues until they die or are relegated to the scrap pile. Usually the longer a Curb stock is held by a purchaser, the less valuable it becomes. Low-priced Curb stocks should never be bought, but if bought, should be sold when a fair profit is in sight. To hold such issues indefinitely, generally means loss.

Stocks

There are stocks and stocks. Some are meritorious while others are questionable and still others worthless. To be able to differentiate between what ones have merit or value and what ones have little or no value, requires some market knowledge and judgment. Those issues listed on a Stock Exchange are usually considered as possessing some merit and value, since before they are listed the corporation or company is required by Governors of the Exchange to make a satisfactory report of the assets behind them before they are admitted to the quoted list. Some of the stocks so quoted on the Big Board have their "try outs" on the Curb. That is to say, they have been traded in as Curb issues. It does not follow, however, that all stocks or a considerable percentage of Curb or unlisted issues will eventually be admitted to a regular Stock Exchange. As a matter of fact, only a comparatively few of such stocks ever get beyond the Curb.

Listed Stocks

When a stock is admitted to the list of stocks quoted and traded in on the N. Y. Stock Exchange it is considered "respectable" and fairly safe to handle after going through a seasoning process. Before being listed, the corporation or company must file with the Governors of the Exchange such data as will enable them to determine whether or not it is eligible for such listing.

It does not necessarily follow that the approval of a stock by the N. Y. Stock Exchange guarantees its quoted price or its value. Stocks may gain or lose in value and price after being listed. All stocks are speculative. No common stocks should be considered as an investment. They are not redeemable by the company or corporation issuing them. The purchaser accepts them *caveat emptor.* If he buys such stocks he takes the chances of their advancing above or declining below what he paid for them. If he buys active stocks at the inception of an upward swing in the market, his chances for speculative profits are at the maximum. If, on the other hand, he buys them after they have had an extended and substantial rise, then his chances for profits diminish in proportion to the advance until they are at the minimum. The prices of stocks are not regulated by their dividend rate. Some stocks with no dividend attached sell higher than stocks paying dividends, while others paying a smaller rate sell higher than those paying a higher rate. There is generally a reason for this anomaly. A stock may have a dividend rate of say 5% and it may be selling on the board at a price to yield 6% or 7% on the investment, or it may be quoted at a price to yield 4%. In the first instance, its present price may be at the end of a substantial downward swing, or it may be caused by uncertainty as to whether the present dividend rate is likely to be continued, or reduced. In the second illustration it may be at or near the top of an extended or substantial upward swing, say in a bull market, or on the probability of an increase in the dividend rate.

Stock Brokers

A stock broker is one who acts as agent for another for the purchase or sale of stocks or bonds.

Not all of those who hold themselves out as stock brokers are legitimate or regular brokers. The term broker is a misnomer when used by a certain class of fellows who "bucket" their customers' trades; so it behooves the person who is about to open an account with a broker, to make inquiry as to the reputation, reliability, integrity and financial responsibility of a broker before depositing his money with him. If the broker be a member of the N. Y. Stock Exchange, the chances are he is reliable and responsible. If he is a member of some other established and regular Exchange, then it is perhaps advisable to look into his financial standing and past record before opening an account with him. If he is not a member of any Exchange, then one must be guided by his financial standing and past record and present methods of conducting business. There are some reliable brokers who are not members of any Exchange. Such brokers deal principally in bonds. The non-members who handle all kinds of stocks are not such brokers as could be recommended to any trader or investor. Nearly all of such brokers, I believe, "bucket" a large percentage of their customers' trades. Even though they do a legitimate business, they are obliged to do it through a broker who is a member of some Exchange. The regular Exchange member charges the non-Exchange member full commission for executing the trade and this is added to the commission which the non-member exacts from his customer, so that the customer really pays a double commission.

It is my opinion that those non-members (and some members) who advertise themselves rather extensively, do considerable "bucketing." There is another class of brokers that does business on the Partial Payment Plan. This is ordinarily a euphemism for bucketing. This plan is looked upon with disfavor by experienced operators. Perhaps not more than ½ of one per cent of such brokers are honest with their clients. The Partial Payment Plan naturally impresses the sophisticated speculator as being a bucket shop operation. These brokers lead their customers to believe that they may buy a stock on what they term a 10 or 20 payment plan, i. e., that after the customers have made all of these payments, the stocks will be delivered full paid—to the customers. Some of them are rash enough to assure the would-be victims—I mean customers that after the first instalment is paid, they will not again be called upon until the next regular instalment becomes automatically due. This seems fair to the lamb and better than buying on margin since in the case of a stock bought on margin and the stock declining, say 7 points, the broker sends out a "S. O. S." call for additional margin, and if the customer fails to respond, his stock is sold out at the market price. The Partial Payment buyer does not take into account that in 95% of transactions, the P. P. broker does not buy the stock his customer ordered to be bought, but buckets it, i. e., takes a chance on it declining much farther before materially higher, and he is generally safe in assuming such a risk, since novices usually buy stocks after they have had a substantial rise. Now, should the stock the customer "bought" decline about 10 points, the P. P. P. broker notifies the customer to deposit the second 10% forthwith. If he hesitates and claims that under the contract the second instalment is not yet due, he is soon thereafter notified that his stock was sold out. If, however, he responds with the second instalment, then the broker buys the stock "at the market" on the assumption that the customer will continue to pay to the end. This operation gives him about 10 points profit on his customer's trade. Now, suppose after the customer bought the stock, it advances 10 or more points and remains above the purchase price for a considerable period and shows a good profit. At this point the customer decides to pay the balance of the instalments and have the stock delivered. Here is where the P. P. broker usually quits or goes into bankruptcy, particularly so if many of his customers act together at the same time. So, regardless of which way the market goes, the bucket broker always wins and the customer generally loses. It is a case of "heads, I win; tails you lose." Some brokers with a bucket shop propensity will sell short through the Exchange every purchase made by his customers if he believes the market is near the top and is about to reverse its trend. If it goes as he expected, he will make profits. If, however, the price advances substantially higher and he elects not to "fail" then he "switches" his customer into something worthless. That is to say, he creates some sort of fake corporation or company supposed to represent oil or mining property divided into thousands of shares at a nominal price, say $1.00 a share. He then prepares an alluring or enticing circular, pamphlet or prospectus (mis)representing the character of the property and addresses it to his customer. In a personal letter he compliments his prospective victim on the good judgment he exhibited in selecting the regular stock that brought him such excellent profits and then goes on to assure him the stock referred to in the circular or prospectus will soon or eventually sell for 5 or more times the price named in the circular, and besides, will in the near future be quoted on the Broad Street Curb. He tells his victim how anxious he is to have him get in on the "ground floor," and urges him to take on as many shares as his account (principal and profit in the first transaction), will allow. In 75% of such cases, the "sucker" acts on the suggestion of his broker. In a short time thereafter the broker decamps or loses his identity.

Then there is another class of brokers who either exploit their own "creations" or act for promoters of low-priced unlisted or curb issues. These are usually questionable or worthless mining, oil or other popular favorites with the public. Several thousands of dollars are spent in advertising the stuff through the columns of newspapers or by crrculars. When the public has been completely saturated or filled up with these questionable or worthless issues, then the advertising campaign is called off. The result is that the market for the worthless stuff becomes stale and the price of the stock declines, perhaps to zero.

There is also the swindling broker who suggests that his prospective customer sell his Liberty Bonds and invest the proceeds in the worthless stocks the broker is promoting and selling, or he may offer to accept from his prospective victim his Liberty Bonds at their face value in payment for the "paper" he has for sale. It is indeed surprising how easy it is to sell the average inexperienced and credulous victim low-priced, unlisted stocks. He "takes a chance" in a game with the odds 100 to 1 against him. My advice has always been: Let such stocks alone and keep away from brokers who specialize in them. If such much-advertised stocks are as valuable as represented, why is the company or the corporation issuing them so anxious to dispose of them. Do the Standard Oil companies, Railroad companies, established Copper companies or other reputable and established companies advertise their stocks and solicit purchasers for them? As a rule, the less meritorious the stock, the more money there is spent in exploiting it. The brokers who handle listed or standard issues that have been on the board a sufficient length of time to become seasoned and well distributed, and who are reluctant to buy or sell low-priced unlisted stocks for their clients, are the most reliable of all brokers to do business with. The brokers who specialize in low-priced or questionable issues would better be avoided.

Stock Manipulation

When a corporation or company is about to issue stock, it usually engages the services of a pool to manipulate the shares so that they may be distributed among the outside purchasers. Manipulating new or unseasoned issues is a comparatively easy proceeding, because (1) there is no stock held by the public and (2) it is hazardous to sell such stocks short because there is no floating supply available for borrowing purposes. Besides, there is no stock held and awaiting a favorable opportunity to be liquidated. In short, there is only "blue sky" above. When the shares have been "boosted" to about the price agreed upon by the members of the pools and the corporation or company issuing them, then the general public is invited to participate as share holders. It is a well known fact that the public prefers to buy stocks at the top rather than at the bottom. This human psychological weakness is taken advantage of by the pools or manipulators. Thus it is, the higher a stock advances, the more it is bulled by inspired rumors and the venal newspapers. After a new stock has been manipulated upward to a "dizzy height," it soon thereafter has a sharp reaction proportionate to its previous advance. Again it is taken in hand by a pool and advanced to near or above the point reached on the preceding rise. These movements are for the purpose of attracting the attention of the public. The pool, understanding the psychological effect such movements have on the public mind, continue them until a following large enough to absorb a good portion of all of the shares is attracted; then the pool unloads on these outsiders. With a relaxing of activities of the pool, the stock naturally sags, perhaps to that point from which it started on its upward flight. At this point, the stock may be taken up again by the pool and given another upward swing, but not with the same spirit that characterized the first and second manipulated upward movements, because there were purchasers of the stock at or near top prices on the two preceding upward swings. These holders may decide to convert their stock certificates or paper profits into cash. The pool surmises this state of mind of the outsiders, so acts cautiously when approaching a probable "realizing zone."

III
BONDS

Government Bonds
State Bonds
Municipal Bonds
Railroad Bonds
The Distinction Between Stocks and Bonds
The Difference Between Speculation and Investment

Government Bonds

United States Government Bonds are issued in two forms: Coupon and registered. Coupon bonds are the most popular bonds. They are payable to bearer and pass by delivery without an indorsement. Registered Bonds are preferred to coupon bonds by buyers who wish to hold for long periods and to guard against possible loss of the bonds. Coupon bonds may be converted into registered bonds through the Treasury Department, but this conversion privilege does not work vice versa. However, the registered bonds may be sold through a Stock Exchange and the coupon bonds bought with the proceeds. The Government does not undertake to protect the actual owner of a coupon bond, while it does in the case of a registered bond. Government bonds are considered the safest class of bonds issued.

State Bonds

These are obligations issued by a state for various purposes—public buildings, public improvements, etc. They usually bear a low rate of interest.

Municipal Bonds

These are issued by cities, counties, boroughs, school districts, etc., generally for gas or water works, sewers, bridges, roads, public buildings and other local improvements. The large cities issue them in both coupon and registered form. They are considered safe investments provided they are the obligations of the entire municipality issuing them, and not a mere part thereof, and provided further that such municipality is permanent and has been incorporated for 10 or more years. The rate of interest is usually low.

Railroad Bonds

Coupon Bond—This is a transferable obligation with a certificate attached whereby the issuer of the bond agrees to pay to bearer a certain sum of money at a named date, i. e., at maturity.

Adjustment Bond

A bond or mortgage given to secure additional funds, usually for improvements or extensions, and ranking subsequent to old liens except on new property.

Collateral Trust Bond or Secured Notes

These are secured by a deposit in trust for security, like bonds or stocks, for the benefit of the bond holders. In case of default, the collateral deposited could be sold for the benefit of the stock holders. They are not considered first-class bonds. They are a sort of debenture bonds, and sometimes referred to as trust certificates.

Consolidated Bond

A bond in which various descriptions of bonds are consolidated.

Convertible Bonds

These are issued by Railroads with the privilege of converting bonds into stock at a named price. They are a sort of " Call " (See Puts and Calls). They may be considered as a second-grade investment.

Debenture Bond

This is an instrument secured by a floating charge junior to other charges secured by fixed mortgages. It is usually secured by a group of securities held in trust (for the benefit of the debenture holders). Such a bond is without a mortgage lien and lacks the power of foreclosure proceedings. The interest on a debenture depends upon the earnings of the corporation issuing the obligation. It is a little better than an Income Bond.

Equipment Notes and Car Trusts

These are in effect a chattel mortgage. They are issued to pay for equipment furnished Railroads and are payable in instalments, usually at the rate of about 10% a year. They are considered good securities. (Those issued under the " Phila. Plan " are considered the best.)

Extension Bonds

These are obligations sometimes issued by a Company unable to pay at maturity. The Company issuing such bonds is considered a weak debtor.

Income Bonds

These are bonds secured by a lien on the net income of the Company. They are obligations on which the issuing Company is obliged to pay interest unless actual net income of the Company is not equal to the amount required for interest. The relation of such a bond to the Company issuing it is about the same as a preferred stock, except that in the case of the Bond, the date of maturity is named. While they are called bonds, they are really not bonds in the real acceptation of the term and are not considered first-class securities. In short, they are promises to pay. The holders, however, come ahead of the general creditors in case of foreclosure.

Industrial Bonds

These securities are based on the plants and the business or productivity of industries of various kinds. They are fairly good security when the products may be classed as essentials or staples having a continuous demand.

Mortgage Bond

This is a promise to pay a specified sum at a named date and with interest at a stated rate and is secured by a mortgage covering all or part of the Company's property. In default of either the principal or the interest, the mortgage can be foreclosed and then sold for the benefit of the holders.

First Mortgage Bond

Is an obligation issued by a company or corporation secured by a first mortgage on all of the real estate and property owned by the Company issuing the bond.

Second Mortgage

This is a junior obligation, secured in the same way as the First Mortgage bond, but subject to the payment of the First. If the First Mortgage is small compared with the security behind it, then the second may be considered safe, and even third and fourth mortgages may be fairly safe if the preceding obligations are for comparatively small amounts.

General Mortgage

An obligation for the benefit of the road as a whole and not for any special department.

Receivers' Certificates

These are notes issued by a receiver of a corporation. They are considered good, but as no definite maturity date is attached to them, they are not considered desirable obligations to hold.

Refunding Bond

This is a financial operation by which the Corporation changes the terms of an interest-bearing debt. It is usually referred to as a conversion. That is to say, the bond then in existence is to be cancelled upon the issuance of a new bond covering the same property. This is often done where the corporation is unable to satisfy or pay the debt at maturity.

Temporary Certificate

This is issued in lieu of permanent obligations to be issued later on.

Terminal Bonds

These securities are issued by several companies jointly to build a terminal for joint use. Their value depends on the strength of the companies issuing them.

Serial Bonds or Notes

Issues for various purposes, redeemable at different specified dates. They are usually designated series, A, B, C, etc.

Unsecured Notes

These are simple obligations issued by a company or corporation to pay the principal and interest of the loan. The holder's rights are subject to prior liens on the property of the corporation or company issuing them. These obligations generally run for a short period and are likely to be paid when due.

There are some other forms of bonds issued, but the foregoing described obligations are the principal issues. The value of a bond is determined by (1) the security behind it; (2), the rate of interest it carries; (3), the date of its maturity. In buying a bond, the purchaser should consider (a), safety; (b), the length of time to maturity; (c), salableness or marketableness. When buying long-term bonds, buy the safest issues—Government, municipal and first mortgage bonds are of this class of securities.

A general list of the various issues of bonds, together with prices and interest rates, may be found in the financial section of the leading metropolitan daily newspapers, either in the Saturday or Sunday editions. A glance over the list will give the reader a comprehensive idea of the difference in prices, even of those in the same classification and bearing the same interest rate. A perusal of the list will prove instructive to the reader.

The Distinction Between Stocks and Bonds

The principal distinction between a bond holder and a stock holder is that the bond holder is a creditor and the stock holder is a part owner. The bond holder lends his money to the company and is promised interest at a stated rate and a repayment of the principal at a future named date. The stock holder has a certain undivided share in the property of the company; a right to participate in profits, and usually voting privileges. The stock holder has the right to a proportionate share of the property after all claims against the property have been satisfied.

Preferred Stock

This issue ranks ahead of the common stock. Its preferences refer to dividends or other assets. There may be 1st, 2nd and 3rd preferred stocks. They rank in the numerical order of issue. The dividends on the preferred must be paid before the common stock receives any dividend. A cumulative dividend designates a dividend or interest which if not paid or received when due, is added to what is to be paid in the future. When buying common stock in any company avoid the unseasoned or newly-listed issues and don't be induced to buy stocks merely because they seem "cheap." If they are low-priced unlisted, or Curb issues, avoid them as you would a man with a police record, since the chances are they are questionable or perhaps worthless. At best, they are hazardous gambles. The chances are if you put your money in these issues, it will never come back to you. Nearly all of the brokers or dealers who specialize in such questionable issues are disreputable characters whose pictures are either in the Rogues Gallery or should be there.

The Difference Between Speculation and Investment

These two terms are different in meaning as applied to purchases of stocks and bonds. An investment is the purchase of Government, State or Municipal bonds or of some other obligation secured by property. Purchases of some stocks are quasi-investments, but all such purchases are more or less speculative, depending upon the basis and management of the Company issuing the stock. Genuine investments are purchases of secured obligations payable at a named date with interest or dividends payable at stated dates until maturity. Stocks, on the other hand, are not redeemable by the Company issuing them.

SPECULATION—The act of buying shares, etc., in expectation of selling at a higher price, or of selling (short) with the expectation of purchasing at a lower price. Any business venture involving unusual risks, with chances of large profits.

INVESTMENT (in stocks or bonds) is the purchase of shares or of bonds in which the element of chance is supposed to be at the minimum, and from which quick or big profits are not anticipated through an advance in price of the stock or bond. Such ventures are usually based on the dividend or interest return.

Some so-called investments are quite speculative, especially so when the dividend or interest rate is high. The higher the rate of income, the more hazardous the investment. Some classes of bonds are safer than most other investments but the designation bond does not always insure its safety as an investment. (See further under the caption Investment and Speculation.)

Stocks are often referred to as "investment securities." Some of them may be fairly good investments, but none of them is a first rate security. They are seldom made to read "redeemable," etc. All bonds are supposed to be redeemable and to have a redemption clause named in them. When you make a so-called investment in stocks, do not let a sense of false security keep you from watchfulness. Besides, keep your eye on the price (if listed on the Stock Exchange) and consult Rule 3 occasionally. It will measure the safety or lack of safety of the stock or stocks you may be interested in. Always be willing to accept a small loss when Rule 3 indicates a further decline, and don't fail to sell such "securities" when they show you good profits, or when the public is clamoring for them. It's generally good business policy to sell when everybody wants to buy, and to buy when nobody wants to buy. Stocks and commodities are usually more attractive to the public when at top prices than when at bargain prices.

IV

HOW INSIDERS AND SKILLED OPERATORS SPECULATE

How the Public Speculates

Now, let us see how the so-called Insiders, pools and skilled operators play the speculative game—first as to the Insiders—these are the big interests who control the market. After they have beaten prices down to such a level that liquidation of the public is about completed, they begin to operate for the upward swing. You know that when a structure is razed for the purpose of erecting a new one on its site, the first thing to be done is to remove the debris of the former structure and establish a clear and solid foundation for the succeeding one. Now, these Insiders work on the same plan. They arrange with the banks to furnish the capital necessary to finance a speculative structure. In other words, they co-operate with the financial institutions because it is necessary to have easy money in order to bull the market for a big swing upward. Usually the venal press at this stage gives out rather pessimistic utterances for the purpose of discouraging outside buying, because the Insiders do not want the public to buy at or near the bottom. However, if the market has advanced on an average of say, 10 points or more in the active issues, then optimistic rumors are set afloat. These utterances are made in the financial section of the newspapers that are co-operating with the Insiders. Of course, this is all inspired stuff and paid for by the Insiders. At this point, the Insiders who bought near the bottom levels take some profits. That is to say, unload some of their holdings on the outsiders that have been induced to come into the market. A reaction of about one-half of the previous advance sets in and then on this reaction the Insiders buy again for another upward swing of 10 or more points. After the list has advanced substantially, a stock here and there makes a spectacular flight upward. This operation serves as a signal for the public to come into the game. Such tactics excite the cupidity and avaricious predilections of the outsiders. When they begin to come in and buy liberally, more profit taking is resorted to by the Insiders and another reaction follows after they have unloaded part of their holdings. At the bottom of this reaction, these Insiders load up again and repeat the process of advancing after reactions until the final culmination of the bull movement. By the time the market has reached its final stages in the upward direction the general public has been lured in and is "buying its head off." The outsiders who have made money on the upward or bull movement boast of their successes in beating the game. This bragging serves to entice their friends and acquaintances into the game. These eleventh-hour "lambs" are of course desirous of emulating their successful blustering friends, so they "invest," with the result that they all soon thereafter lose their "fleeces." When the market has reached the culmination point at the top and the Insiders have marketed their stocks and gone short, it sometimes so happens that the public comes in stronger than the Insiders anticipated and prices are carried beyond the point to which these Insiders had planned for them to go. In short, the public has taken the market machinery out of the hands of the Insiders; so something must be done to make it release its hold. The first thing usually done in such a situation is to increase the call rate of money to a high rate and so frighten the outsiders. If this does not bring the desired result, then something "happens" that frightens the outsiders into selling out. This selling causes a sharp, perhaps drastic set-back of many points; in fact, far enough to dislodge most of the outsiders who have bought on the way up. The stocks the outsiders are obliged to sell in order to save themselves from large losses or from having exhausted margins, the Insiders buy to cover the shorts they put out near the culmination point at the top. After the "slaughter of the innocents" or the "fleecing of lambs," the general market swings back, usually about one-half of its decline and on this upward swing the Insiders put out more short lines of stock. This operation finished, they then beat down the list until all of the vulnerable accounts of the outside buyers have been exhausted or wiped off the brokers' books. The Insiders have indirect secret access to the accounts of the clients, through the brokers' books, so they know about how far they must depress prices in order to exhaust all of the vulnerable margined accounts. Every movement is made with a view to beat the outsiders. That is what the game is for, and of course this organized force, constituting the Insiders, is capable of doing such things.

The same tactics and strategy employed in playing the stock game is resorted to in the commodity markets—Cotton, Wheat, Corn, Oats and Provisions. New York and New Orleans are the headquarters for operating in cotton, and Chicago for grain and provisions. The Windy City operators are a pretty slick crew and manage to fool the outside public to a greater degree than does the Stock Exchange market crowd. The Chicago false rumor works and the "news factory" are always busy during market hours, and on some occasions they work overtime. Any person who speculates in grain or provisions and who accepts or places credence in or relies on any reports or "news" emanating from Chicago respecting grain or provisions, is likely to "lose his shirt." Speculation in grain and provisions is perhaps more uncertain than in stock for the unskilled speculator, because he is apt to rely on "news" and rumors for his guidance. The unwary, credulous and unsophisticated trader who depends on such false "guides" in making his commitments is engaged in a losing venture.

One should treat the Chicago market as a game, pure and simple. If you are influenced by what you may read or hear, or what is sent by telegrams during the market hours, you are almost certain to lose. The reason so few succeed in operating in grain and provisions is that they do what the Chicago crowd seeks to influence them to do. This clique is made up of provision packers, crop experts and profiteers who prey upon the outside public. The highwayman is respectable compared with some of these fellows. The cotton crowd of manipulators is not so disreputable as they were in 1910-11 when they cornered the cotton market. An outsider has little chance in playing the cotton game unless he puts wax in his ears and plays the game according to the Rules set forth on other pages of this book. That the speculative game is the same old game and is played in the same old way, the reader is invited to read the following, which I wrote and circulated in 1910:

Can the Game Be Beaten?

To the question whether the Wall Street game can be beaten, the answer may truthfully be given both affirmatively and negatively; it all depends on how it is played. To beat it continuously one must possess special mental equipment, *i. e.*, have natural aptitude for speculation.

Every person is not temperamentally or mentally endowed to be a successful speculator any more than is every one to become a successful writer, an inventor, a financer, an educator, or to excel in every line of physical or mental activity. Some persons are perennial optimists, others are natural pessimists. The former are always Bulls, the latter persistent Bears.

Now, both of these are temperamentally unfitted to become successful speculators, because they are apt to see only one side of a condition, only one side of a market.

One requires a mind that can see both sides of a question or a condition—needs a sort of judicial mind, if you please. The general public is naturally a Bull, and therefore wrong marketwise at least half of the time. The higher a market soars, the more bullish the public becomes, the more anxious to participate in the game for a still further rise.

The lower it recedes, the less interest it takes in prices or quotations—the less desirous to purchase—the more anxious to liquidate holdings. This is one reason why the public pays the expenses incident to running the game.

If people would use the same judgment, and employ the same methods they are accustomed to do in their regular business or enterprises or everyday affairs, they could make money in the stock and commodity markets. While speculation is not gambling *per se*, it is so to the person who knows nothing about the game. If he be ignorant of the strategy and tactics employed to advance or depress quotations; of the skill used in circulating rumors calculated to stimulate buying, or cause selling; of the probable effect of a given event on values, then he is a gambler, pure and simple.

Gamblers as a rule are bad speculators, *i. e.*, unsuccessful; the same observation applies with equal force to plungers and crooks. "Why is this so?" The gambler usually bases his commitment on mere chance, impulse, rumor or "inside information."

The plunger generally plays rashly and against good judgment. While he may occasionally make what is termed a "killing," the chances are that he will ultimately wind up his speculative ventures with losses. There are, however, occasions when a man of good judgment, and who knows the rules of the game, may take a plunge, but even with such an advantage, it's hazardous to play the exception rather than the rule. Crooks or dishonest men can not have lasting success in speculative ventures, because their mental vision is distorted; they see things twisted and upside down.

The well balanced, upright speculator, who usually sees things as they are or as they are likely to be, is the most apt to succeed in speculation.

"How is it possible to succeed in Wall Street?" Well, here are a few hints that should guard him against the pitfalls leading to failure or disaster, and some suggestions that if followed, should enable a man possessing a fair share of common sense, to make the game as safe and legitimate as any other enterprise in which the element of trading enters.

In the first place, he must determine whether he is operating in, or about to operate in, a Bull or a Bear market—*i. e.*, whether it is inclined upward or downward. This point may be settled by looking over the history of the market covering a period of a month or more. If the average of prices during that time shows an ascending scale, *i. e.*, indicates the tide rising a little higher on each successive wave, then he is justified in concluding the market is a Bull affair and that it should be bought on sharp recessions. If, on the other hand, the average of prices running back over a like period shows each wave reacting lower than the preceding one, and the rallies or rebounds fall short of the former one, then he is justified in concluding it is a Bear market, so should be sold on the rebounds or rallies. In the case of a Bull market, if he is playing for more than daily profits, in other words for substantial gains, he holds his long trades until the list has advanced to that point where buoyancy and more than ordinary animation and volume of transactions are in evidence. At such a point the whole list usually participates in the forward movement and the leaders add as much to their price on this day as in the two or three preceding ones combined, and do much backing and filling consequent upon the manipulation by the Bulls to liquidate or distribute their holdings. Incidentally, close observers will doubtless notice one or two normally inactive shares shooting upward. This is one of those tricks peculiar to the game—practiced for the purpose of deceiving the other fellows. With these symptoms in evidence the prudent outsider will do a little liquidating on his own account and if he be possessed of some skill will sell a moderate number of shares short for moderate profits. Now, he will wait until the list has a material setback or reaction, then act as do the manipulators who brought about the reaction, viz., purchase for another rise. This reaction or setback usually extends to about midway between the high point from which the decline started, and the point from which it began after the preceding reaction.

At this point there is generally the animation and irregularity that characterized the market at the point of distribution, but the object is the reverse, *i. e.*, it's for accumulation for another forward swing.

Now, if when the list nears the top of the former high wave, there be the signs in evidence as before this last reaction, then the holder of long stock would better let the other fellows have it. If, however, the list goes forward in an orderly way and averages a substantial fraction above the former high, then he is justified in concluding that the leaders are going materially higher, and will hang on and wait for that animation or buoyancy that gives him the signs of a culmination in the movement.

In a Bear market the operation is reversed, with this difference, that at the end of each downward swing, there is more irregularity and demoralization than at the finish of a reaction in a Bull market, followed by a violent rebound, when the selling pressure is released.

Never to buy a Bear market, or sell a Bull market, is a pretty safe rule to follow, unless one be a skilled speculator. Nevertheless, good profits may often be obtained through purchases made at the point of demoralization in a Bear market, but such operations should be backed by liberal margins.

"About what margin should be used in all these operations?" Well, for those who are not professionals, about 20 points margin should be behind every commitment.

Some persons use what are termed "stop loss" orders, *i. e.*, to close out the trade if it touches a designated price. A large percentage of traders make the stop loss price as near as ½ to 1 point from the buying or selling price, but such close stops to save losses savor of gambling, and in the end show so many losses that they are liable to overbalance profits. The use of close stops may serve the purpose of exchange members who pay no commission on trades, but for the outsider it's generally suicidal financially, unless he knows most of the rules governing the game.

There's a class of investors or speculators who make their commitments on the dividend yield basis. This is an erroneous method for determining the merits of stocks, as any one may readily realize by going over the securities listed on the New York Stock Exchange. Dividends are sometimes advanced, reduced or passed for speculative purposes.

"What constitute the qualifications necessary for success in speculation?" There are four principal ones, and their relative value is in about this order: 1st, Judgment or knowledge; 2d, Nerve; 3d, Money; 4th, Patience. In some respects nerve ranks first as a necessary quality, but this inherent asset without judgment to direct it is as liable to lead its possessor in the wrong as in the right direction. However, without nerve one can accomplish little in speculative ventures. A man may have judgment, but if he lack nerve he will not make a howling success as a speculator. But judgment is necessary. It is the pilot that directs the mind past the financial rocks, sand bars and threatened dangers on the sea of speculation; so we see this element combined with nerve makes a strong combination for success.

Money is the least important of all the essentials in the game, since with a good stock of nerve, backed by good judgment, a small amount of capital may be increased indefinitely.

Patience is a valuable asset. It enables one to wait until a favorable opportunity presents itself to get in and to get out of the market.

No person other than a member of the Exchange should make daily trades, because the commissions are likely to eat up the profits and perhaps the capital besides; so, too, the trader who accepts fractional profits and large losses is apt to lose all he puts into the game.

The man who buys close to the top or sells very near to the bottom, takes big chances. It's natural for a trader to follow the crowd in speculation, as in other matters, but such a policy is usually erroneous, since the crowd is generally going when the knowing ones are coming, and vice versa.

When the public is buying its head off, or selling out at bargain prices, then is the opportunity for the man with a liberal margin to sell what the public is anxious to buy at any price, and to buy what it is frantic to sell regardless of price. The successful speculator guards against being influenced by "news" and rumors intended to mislead the public. It requires a fine sense of discernment to detect the difference between real news and the spurious article.

From what has heretofore been observed concerning speculation we are led to believe the game can be beaten if a speculator exercise fairly good judgment, possesses common sense and has regard for the principles and rules that govern market movements. But it can't be beaten by the person who imagines speculation a gamble or a guess and plays it on that theory, for market movements are not haphazard affairs. They are governed by certain laws and there are rules for acting in harmony with these laws, but the rank and file are not supposed to know or understand them any more than is the private soldier expected to know the tactics, strategy and science of warfare. At best, Wall Street is not an easy game to beat.

The Street gives grudgingly any but hard earned dollars, so if you are looking for "easy money," you'll have to look elsewhere for it.

How the Public Speculates

Unskilled, inexperienced or unsophisticated speculators in stocks or commodities make their commitments on a hit or miss plan. Let us see how the various "outsiders" (the public) think and act in buying and selling stocks and commodities. Let us examine the workings of the minds of some of these outsiders, in their relation to buying and selling stocks and commodities. Persons with little or no practical knowledge of speculation and unable to differentiate between the meritorious and the worthless stocks may read the advertisements in the newspapers setting forth in glowing terms the extraordinary opportunities offered the public. The prices are from one cent to $1 or more a share. These shares will soon be selling at 5 to 10 times or more than their present price (according to the flowery and luring announcement). They represent oil wells or mines, actual or "invisible"—principally the latter. The unwary are thus lured into buying the stuff.

Then, too, the average unskilled trader, when he sees the general market advancing, is anxious to get into the current and go with it, so he glances along the list of stocks on the board for the name of some stock that he imagines gives promise of an advance. He selects one and buys it; soon thereafter to his great surprise, he sees the stock he bought decline instead of advance. He has acted on the erroneous theory that when the general list shows advances, all stocks will advance. He has not yet learned that though the averages of the general list show upward, or show downward, there are always one or more stocks indicating a trend in the opposite direction. Here's where the man who can read the tape and plays according to the Rules is "at home" in the game. Another mistake the unskilled trader is wont to make: He sees a stock advance or decline on active trading. Instead of operating in this stock, the leader, he buys or sells another in the same group expecting it to follow the leader. Always operate in the leader. Buy it when it is advancing; sell it when declining.

Unskilled speculators are prone to buy a stock or commodity because it seems "cheap" and to sell a stock when it seems "too high." The fact is a stock or commodity is seldom too low to sell short, or too high to buy. Caution, however, should be exercised in buying after a big advance, or selling after a drastic decline.

If a man were to apply for employment as a carpenter, engineer, brick-layer, plumber, etc., it would be presumed by the person solicited that the applicant had served an apprenticeship of 2 or more years in order to qualify him for the job sought. So an applicant for any employment requiring more or less skill and experience would likely be questioned as to his past performances and qualifications before being taken on. If, in all of the above supposed cases it should be found that the applicant had no experience, his application would likely be treated as presumptious.

In entering upon speculative ventures, or in making investments, the average person does not seemingly consider it necessary to have had some previous experience in such matters, although more skill is necessary for success therein than in almost any other vocation or calling requiring mental qualifications. The average inexperienced speculator seems to imagine that it's all a matter of luck and that knowledge plays only a minor or a negligible part in the operations. Such a speculator does not stop to consider the fact that speculation is a scientific game and that he is trying to match his wits against the skill of men possessing trained mental alertness, combined with experience and an abundance of financial resources. The public is to such a force what a mob would be in a contest with a body of Federal soldiers under orders.

The average novice, and even he who has had a "haphazard" experience in the speculative game, knows little of the dangers that lurk therein while trying to speculate successfully without knowing something definite about the laws of market movements. There are those who have had experience in the market, but who never seem to realize that the movements are more than mere chance ones, so they act on the assumption that speculative commitments may be made on "news," impulse, opinion, judgment, information, rumor, etc., and that these will bring desired results. Operations in the market predicated on this false theory bring failure. Such a plan of operations may prove successful temporarily but in the end financial disaster will come. Everything works in harmony with certain laws and these laws are immutable and work out logically in spite of what we may believe or disbelieve or fail to understand. To succeed in any line of effort, we must act in harmony with these laws and if we fail so to do, a penalty is exacted, and in the case of stock speculation—financial failure naturally follows. Few persons realize the power of mental suggestion regardless of its source. Low-priced issues seem to appeal strongly to those who have had little experience. This may come from an idea that (1) such a stock cannot decline far; (2) its chance for advancement is good; (3) a given capital will buy more of that particular stock than it would of one selling higher in price. They do not seem to take into account that when a stock is selling low, there is some particularly good reason why it is quoted at such a price. Then, too, inexperienced speculators are inclined to buy stocks after they have advanced substantially and perhaps to near their top prices. Stocks seem to be more attractive then than when they were selling at a much lower price. This erroneous opinion or theory is usually the result of unconscious mental suggestion brought about by inspired articles or comments set forth in the financial columns of venal newspapers or financial periodicals or from circular letters, or from what they may have heard observed by their acquaintances. There seems to be in the minds of the average persons a desire to see prices of stocks advance. The higher they go, the more attractive they appear, so we find that when the market has reached its apex, there is usually more buying than at any point of its upward movement. This is the danger point and here are the rocks on which the speculators' financial craft is usually wrecked. Any ordinary seaman can sail a boat in fair weather and in a favorable breeze, but when a storm arises, or when a rocky coast is approached, the services of an experienced navigator are required to save the ship, the passengers and crew from destruction. Few inexperienced speculators realize the dangers that threaten them when the market has advanced substantialy and is about to culminate or turn from an upward to a downward course. Usually such persons lose all they have made on the upward swing through lack of knowledge of such dangers. If the market be a bull market, they buy on every reaction and perhaps take profits from time to time and then reinstate trades. They repeat the operation—each time increasing the size of their commitments. That is, they add the profits already made to their capital and continue to buy as before, so when the market reaches the top they are using their capital to the limit. The reverse movement that is about to set in, they do not know about and so do not anticipate it; thus it is that after a reaction of considerable extent they find themselves unable to protect their last commitments and as a result their stock or stocks are sold out by their brokers at the market, usually near the bottom. So in a bear market, the same methods are pursued by others whose predilections favor the short side. We thus find these two sets of traders—one buying at the top—the other selling short at the bottom of swings. Of course, the result is the same in both instances—disastrous.

Then there is that other sort of speculator: He decides to take an active part in the market and then selects some particular stock to buy. This decision is based on reading or hearing something that seems to favor the prospective purchase he has in mind. He reads all the "dope" he finds laid out for him in brokers' offices. He consults with his friends—or perhaps his brokers. He asks Jim, Jack and Bill for their opinions. They all coincide with him in that what he has decided upon is the right thing to do. Now, after being filled up with conclusive proof that his decision is justified, he buys, only to find a little later on that he has selected the wrong stock; that instead of going up it declines, but he is not discouraged so he buys some more on a decline—to average up. This is termed averaging. The initial trade was made on the theory that the stock bought would advance, but having failed so to do he makes a second trade on a decline of two or three points; the stock still recedes; he buys again lower down. Ultimately he is likely to lose all on the trades he has made, particularly so if the stock declines further than he anticipated it to go. The theory that one ill-advised trade can be made good by making two or three more of the same kind seldom works out—profitably. He perhaps does not realize that the trend has changed since he bought, and instead of buying again as he did he should have gone with the trend, that is, he should have taken a small loss on his first commitment and then sold "short" in anticipation of a further decline. As a general rule, the inexperienced trader makes a trade that is easy for him to make. Usually such trades go wrong. The fact is, that the harder it is to make a trade, the greater is the probability of reaping a profit on such a commitment.

Another mistake that the average unskilled trader makes is in expecting more than reasonable profits. He is not satisfied with a reasonable profit, so waits for more. This greed is the cause of more severe losses, marketwise, than almost any other weakness. A trader sees the general market advance. He finds by consulting figures or a chart that the trend of the average of price shows upward and he decides to buy something. After looking over the board he concludes to take on a stock that has seemingly been overlooked in, the upward movement in the general list so he buys that stock and is chagrined to find out later that it is declining instead of advancing. This mystifies him. Now the fact is, that in a genuine bull market, when the composite average shows upward day after day, there are always one or more stocks showing a trend downward, so if these are bought, a loss is likely to result. The same movement may be noticed when the trend of the general market is downward and the average list shows losses from day to day; one or more stocks will be showing an upward trend, so in both of these cases the unskilled trader is likely to go wrong—by buying in the first instance and selling in the second. These exceptional movements in an upward trend and in a downward trend are sometimes tactical and for the purpose of deceiving the outside public. They may be likened to military tactics or strategy when one army desires to retreat, and to cover such retreat, makes a big demonstration on the right and left flanks of the enemy. Sometimes when the bulls are taking profits at or near the top of the market they advance a stock here and there for the purpose of diverting attention of the outsiders from the real operations of the Insiders. These are tactical operations and intended to deceive the public.

It is a fact that a man is naturally disposed to listen to suggestions or accept advice agreeable to his inclination, wishes or interests, regardless of their source or their soundness. Advices or suggestions not in harmony with his opinions or his interests are usually unacceptable and are usually ignored even though they be sound and correct. Human nature has changed little during the past 10,000 years.

Many traders are misled by large transactions. If they see a stock advance ⅛ or ¼ on a 1,000, 2,000, 3,000 share lot the are instantly convinced that that particular stock is on the way to a higher price and thus are influenced to buy it. Now, as a matter of fact, these large lots may have been covering of shorts and not purchases for an anticipated further advance. Buying or selling based on the theory that large transactions indicate the trend for further higher or lower prices is misleading. The fact is that 100 share lots signify more marketwise than thousand share lots, in that quotations may be made on 100 share lots followed by transactions in larger lots for anticipated profits in the opposite direction. This is usually the case when the tape records 1,100, 1,600, 2,100, 2,600, 3,100. In such quotations, the 100 share lot transaction is used to make the market for the larger lot. For selling purposes, the seller bids 1/8 above the last sale, then follows with a sale of a 1,000, 2,000, 3,000, etc. The size of the transactions are unreliable market guides, so volume of transactions in a stock or in the market is negligible unless *abnormally* large or abnormally small.

There are traders who are misled by reading some statements in a periodical devoted to odd lots. This publication sometimes gives out statements something like this: "The purchases this week were 50% more than sales." Of course, these commitments are made by odd lot traders, and since the small traders are usually wrong, in making their commitments, the chances are 10 to 1, you may sell the market immediately upon the appearance of such an announcement, with an assurance of good profits.

Still another error: Buying a stock because it seems cheap. Selling a stock because it seems too high. A stock is seldom too low to sell short for a further decline or too high to buy for a further advance. High and low are so by comparison or contrast. Never buy a stock unless the tape shows it is a purchase, nor sell it short when the tape shows its trend upward. Opinion is of little value marketwise. Stocks and commodities have a way of moving opposite to our opinion. A man standing near the ticker was asked his opinion on the market. He replied: "My opinion is, it is going down, but the ticker says up." The tape is a more reliable guide marketwise than opinion, so if your opinion does not coincide with what the ticker indicates, better discard your opinion.

V.

BUYING AND SELLING STOCKS, GRAIN, COTTON, COFFEE, SUGAR, PROVISIONS

Buying and Selling on a Scale or Averaging
Short Selling
Hedging
A Hint to Farmers

Stocks may be bought or sold on margin. They may also be bought outright or on the partial payment plan. The latter plan is favored by brokers who prefer to "bucket" customers' trades. Brokers charge a commission of $7.50 on every 100 shares bought or sold of stocks selling below $10 a share; $15 on stock selling at $10 and below $125 a share; and $20 on stocks selling at $125 or higher. Ten or more points margin is required on buying or selling trades. The brokers charge interest on the purchase price of the stock, less the margin advanced by the customer at the time of purchase. No interest is charged on "short" sales. I always advise against buying stocks on the partial payment plan, and warn the reader against doing business with brokers who do business on such a plan, because such brokers generally "bucket" the transactions, *i. e.*, neither buy nor sell for the customers, but take the risk of anticipating that the customer's trade will result in a loss to the customer, with its corollary—a profit to the bucketeer—equal to the loss suffered by the customer or victim. When stocks are bought at a low level of prices following a drastic decline, buying for cash is usually advisable. The margin plan is preferable in all other cases.

Buying and Selling Grain

Cereals are usually bought and sold on margin. No interest charges are paid during the life of the option.

Elevator or storage charges are reflected in the difference in prices of the options. Buyers of "cash" grain are charged storage. The margin required on Wheat is from 10c. to 30c., and about 5c. to 20c. a bushel on Corn, depending on the fluctuations. The margin required on Oats is less than on Wheat and Corn because the fluctuations are usually narrower. A regular trade on the Chicago Board of Trade is 5,000 bushels. This corresponds with 50 shares of stock on the Stock Exchange, *i. e.*, the profits or losses on a transaction covering the same number of fractions would be about the same, less the difference in commissions and other charges incident to the trade. $500 to $1,000 is usually required by the broker as margin from the customer making a 5,000-bushel trade. The brokers' commission is $15 for a 5,000-bushel lot for a round turn, that is, for both buying and selling. An advance or decline of 1c. a bushel in grain is equivalent to a dollar advance or decline in a stock in a speculative sense, *i. e.*, the profit or loss would be the same, less the difference in commission and other charges.

Buying and Selling Cotton

This commodity, like grain, is bought and sold on margin. No interest charge attaches. One hundred points represents one cent a pound. One cent a pound is equivalent to $5 a bale, 20 points equal $1 a bale. The broker's commission for a round turn on Cotton is $20 for 100 bales. The broker requires from 40 to 100 points margin on both long and short trades, *i. e.*, for buying for an advance and for selling short for an anticipated fall or decline in price. In active movements, Cotton offers splendid opportunities for making big profits. The speculator in this staple must be proof against "news," opinion, statistics, etc., as in the case of trading in grain. The same Rules apply in Cotton as in grain and stocks because the same law of movements operates alike in stocks, grain and cotton. For the purpose of applying Rule 3, 20 points in Cotton are equivalent to 1 point ($1) in stocks and 1 cent in grain, so a fluctuation of 10 points in Cotton may be considered equal to ½ point in stocks.

Coffee

The unit in this commodity is divided into 100 parts termed points, which represent 1 cent as in Cotton and is traded in as futures.

Sugar

This commodity is divided into 100 points and traded in as in the case of Coffee.

Provisions

Pork—This product is quoted in dollars and cents per barrel and is traded in accordingly, either for cash or as futures on margin.

Lard—This commodity is quoted in dollars and cents and traded in on margin for future delivery.

The general public does not trade in futures in Sugars, Coffee, Pork, Lard, Ribs, and it is perhaps well that it does not, especially so in Pork, Lard and Ribs, since these provisions are so closely held by Insiders and are so easily manipulated against the outsider that it is hazardous to make speculative ventures in them. The unit of Pork is 250 barrels. That of Ribs and Lard 50,000 pounds. The broker's commission charges are $20 for a round turn (both buying and selling) for any of these provisions.

Buying and Selling on a Scale or Averaging

This method of trading or investing is quite prevalent among traders and investors. Commitments made on such an ill-advised plan generally bring financial disaster to those who practice it. Such a plan of action is wrong in its inception. It is predicated on the theory that two or more bad trades make a good one, or cure an original erroneous commitment. For illustration, let us suppose the trader or investor buys a stock at 100 on the theory that after it has declined say 15 points, it is a safe purchase for a rally or an advance. He buys it, but to his surprise it declines, so to rectify his first mistake he buys another lot at 95 to average. It declines to 90; he buys another lot. It still continues to decline and reaches 85; again he buys another lot. The stock fails to rise, but descends to 80. He again takes on another lot. By this time he may have exhausted his capital or is unable to furnish the broker with further margins, so his stock is either sold out by his broker, or the trader orders his broker to sell his holdings at the market. It may easily be imagined how such a trader would have fared had he bought a stock or commodity on the averaging plan, that fell 50 or 100 points below the price at which his initial commitment was made. "Oh," he may say, "such declines do not occur." For proof that they do occur, let him glance over the slumps that occurred in some of the profiteering stocks that were ballooned in the fictitious and artificial Bull market orgy of 1919. Averaging on cereals and cotton in the summer and autumn of 1920 would have proven equally disastrous. So selling short on a scale as these stocks and commodities went skyward would have brought the same disastrous result.

The theory of averaging is based on the assumption that the trader knows when to make his initial trade, The fact that his initial trade was a mistake is proven by his subsequent commitments; so, if he made a mistake in the first instance what logical reason has he to suppose he will not make another in the second, third, fourth, tenth or twentieth trade. A little investigation and the exercise of a fair share of horse sense will blast the averaging theory in market operations.

Now let us see what is the logical and sensible plan for buying or selling on a scale. We have seen from the foregoing examples and explanations that averaging *against* the trend of the stock or commodity is the wrong course. Now, it follows that the correct course of action marketwise is to follow the trend of a stock or commodity and in buying on a scale, purchase on an ascending scale and sell on a descending scale. For example: The trend is upward. A commitment is made at say 60. The stock or commodity advances to 62, buy another lot; it ascends to 64, buy another lot; it rises to 66, buy some more; it goes to 68, buy another lot; now, if it reaches about 70, to which it may be due under the Swing Rule, take profits. As the stock advances from 60, a Stop Loss order should be placed after 64 is reached, say at 62; then raised as the stock or commodity advances. This is the only safe method for buying on a scale. The same principle applies for selling on a scale. In short, always follow the trend with a Stop Loss behind every commitment.

Short Selling

Inexperienced speculators are prone to ask: "How can I sell something I do not own or possess?" Such transactions are made daily by manufacturers and merchants. Let us see how this is done: The merchant buys dry goods from the textile manufacturers in February to be delivered in May. The goods thus bought have not yet been manufactured. The manufacturer has obviously sold something he does not possess, but the chances are the goods will be made up and ready for delivery in accordance with the terms of the sale. The lumber manufacturer sells to a builder or dealer a specified bill of lumber to be delivered on or before a named date. The timber from which the lumber is to be made is still in the tree. The manufacturer has seemingly sold something he does not yet possess. The manufacturer contemplates turning the timber into lumber before the date of delivery to the buyer. The steel manufacturer in May sells certain steel products not yet made up from the raw material. The delivery is to be made in September, or the sale may contemplate immediate delivery. In such a case the steel manufacturer may buy from another manufacturer and thus make an immediate or earlier delivery. The retail merchant may not have in stock the goods a customer desires. Nevertheless, the merchant sells his customer the goods and then buys them from the wholesaler and delivery to the customer is made. The farmer, needing money in the spring after sowing Wheat or planting Cotton, goes to the merchant or to a bank and sells his anticipated crop at a named price to be delivered in October. If the crop does not equal the amount sold, then the farmer must buy enough to make a full delivery according to the terms of the sale. If the price he pays is less than the price at which he sold in the spring, then he makes a profit on such a purchase and if more, then a loss.

A majority of traders favor the buying side of the market. The minority, the selling, or short side. The more experience one has in trading, the more he is inclined to operate on both sides, thus taking advantage of movements in either direction. When a person buys, it is with the expectation that the stock or commodity bought will rise or advance and thus show a profit on the transaction. He expects to be able to sell what he bought, at a higher price than he paid. If he succeeds in so doing, then he makes a profit. If he fails so to do, he loses.

Now, the man who sells short, that is, sells something he does not actually possess at the moment of sale, is impelled by the motive that prompted a purchase for a rise, namely, to obtain an anticipated profit. The person who sells short does so expecting to be able to buy the stocks or commodities sold short, at lower prices than he sold them and thus be able to deliver to the person who bought at a higher price the stocks or commodities contracted to be sold or delivered, in such a transaction. Now if the stocks or commodities sold short decline in price as anticipated by the short seller and he buys them in (covers) at a less price than that at which he sold short, then he has made a profit equal to the difference between the selling price and the price at which he bought—less the broker's commission and taxes. Should, however, the short seller err in his forecast or anticipation of the stocks or commodities he sold short for an expected decline—advance instead beyond the price at which he sold short, then a loss instead of a profit would be indicated, just as would a decline in the stocks or commodities bought for an advance, in case of a decline.

In selling short one must always buy in (cover) that which was sold short, since no delivery can be made until this is done. In short, the transaction is not completed until a sale and delivery. The broker may, however, borrow stocks and deliver them for the short seller and thus defer an actual purchase to cover. So a short sale may run for an indefinite period—days, weeks, months—but ultimately the stock must be bought and delivered. The one advantage of short selling is this—there are no interest charges on a short sale. On commodities like Grain and Cotton there is a limit of time on deliveries both for buyers and sellers, but no carrying or warehouse charges during the life of the option on the commodity bought or sold. For example: If you buy July Wheat or Cotton, say in January, you must deliver them by June 30. If you sell them short you may carry the trade through to July 31, but you must before the life of the option expires, buy in the Grain or Cotton you have sold short.

In 1909 an expert committee to examine the Exchange reported thus on "short selling": "We do not think that it is wrong to agree to sell something that one does not now possess, but expects to obtain later. Contracts and agreements to sell, and deliver in the future, property which one does not possess at the time of the contract, are common in all kinds of business. The man who has 'sold short' must some day buy, in order to return the stock which he has borrowed to make the short sale. * * * Short selling tends to produce steadiness in prices, which is an advantage to the community. No other means of restraining unwarranted marking up and down of prices has been suggested to us."

Hedging

Hedge literally means to shelter one's self from danger or risk. Hedging, as applied to speculative operations, means to reduce the risk of a purchase or a sale of stocks or commodities by making a commitment (purchase or sale) against the purchase or sale one has already made, thus guarding against loss.

Such operations are practiced or entered into by textile manufacturers and millers to guard themselves against possible losses on the purchase of raw materials that enter into the manufactured products. When the cotton manufacturer buys raw cotton for the purpose of converting it into cloth, he must protect himself against the possible changes in the price of cotton between the time of the purchase and the date when the finished product is sold and deliverable. The period that may elapse between the purchase of the raw cotton and the delivery date of the material made from the same, may be weeks or months. In the meantime, the price of cotton may change many points,

i. e., advance beyond or decline below what the manufacturer paid for the raw material. He may have contracted to deliver the cotton at a price that would entail a loss to the manufacturer, owing to an unexpected advance in the price of the raw cotton to be bought to fill the contract with the purchaser of the cloth.

On the other hand, the price of the raw cotton may decline below the price at which it was bought or may be bought to fill the contract based on the higher price current at the time of the sale. In this case, the manufacturer would profit proportionately. The manufacturer cannot afford to do business on such uncertain contingencies. He does not base his purchases and sales on the probable advances or probable declines in his favor. His business is the manufacture of cotton goods and his duty is to safeguard profits and to guard against losses. This he does by hedging.

For illustration: He buys 500 bales of "spot" (cash) cotton to be manufactured into cloth. Immediately thereafter he sells short (hedges) 500 bales of cotton deliverable about the date when the purchased 500 bales are converted into cloth and sold to the merchant. Now, if the price of raw cotton advances, he loses on his short sale. But what he loses there he makes up in profits on the 500 bales he bought to be used in his factory.

Suppose the cotton manufacturer did not take the precaution to insure himself against contingencies? He would be an extremely fortunate man if he did not run into misfortune eventually. In short, he would find himself in the speculator class—taking all the chances incident to such ventures. So, too, the miller when he buys wheat to be converted into flour and the price of wheat declines after the purchase, a loss confronts him, because he must sell the flour made from that wheat at a lower price, i. e., at a price in harmony with the prevailing or current price of wheat.

The primitive method of insuring the miller against contingent losses was to buy grain from the farmer at a price sufficiently lower than what it was worth in order to insure the miller against contingencies in prices of wheat. Of course, this plan militated against the farmer.

It was the case of the white man and the Indian who went out to hunt. Together they killed a turkey and a crow. In dividing up the game, the white man suggested to the Indian, "You take the crow and I'll take the turkey; or I'll take the turkey and you take the crow."

The miller acts in the purchase of grain as does the textile manufacturer in the purchase of raw cotton. Both practically take out insurance policies. This method of doing business enables both to run their business on a closer margin of profits than otherwise.

A Hint to the Farmer

The price of commodities is usually at the highest point either about the planting season or near the period when the crop gathering season is setting in. These are the dates the farmer should watch closely, that he may definitely decide whether he should sell his unharvested or ungathered crop then, or postpone selling until the crop is garnered. The wise farmer will sell before the crops of his neighbors have been harvested and threshed. The farmer innocently asks: "How can I sell my crop of corn, wheat, oats or cotton before it is harvested?" That is easily answered. Sell short (hedge) through a broker an amount equal to your expected crop. Make it deliverable in that option month following the one when you usually garner your crop. This plan will enable you to arrive early and thus avoid the crowd.

VI
CHARTS

Puts and Calls
Futures
The Ticker
Signs and Symptoms
Experience an Expensive Teacher

Charts are diagrams in graphic form for tracing the movements of a stock or commodity or a composite movement embracing several issues in a group, or in several issues of different groups. They serve to show at a glance by tracings, the movements made over a period of days, weeks, months or years. These graphic charts are a record or history of past movements. Since the past and the present make the future, a graphic record of market movements is essential for guidance in making future commitments in the markets. Until a compartively recent date, the chart was unpopular and those who made them or believed in them wrere termed "chart fiends." The unpopularity of charts was perhaps owing to the fact that not over 1 per cent. of those who made them understood their meaning or could read them after they made them. They were to such persons what copying Greek words might be to one who could not read or speak Greek. The chart is now popular with those who know the significance of the tracings and possess knowledge of the laws of market movements. No successful trader ignores charts and all successful traders use them. There may be persons who can retain in their minds past movements in stocks or commodities, but why burden the mind with abstract quotations when they may be pictured? Besides, the memory may not always be depended upon. Does a person doing a considerable volume of business rely on his memory for a record of transactions, or does he record them in a book or set of books?

A composite chart of say 25 industrials, if industrials are the active issues, will give you approximately the points to which swings of the speculative pendulum will likely reach in their upward and downward direction in both major and minor or intermediate movements. You are thus enabled to determine approximately the point to which the swing of Industrials will extend and the reverse movement set in. The same result may be obtained and determined in a chart embracing say 15 railroad stocks. Of course a rail chart will apply to a swing in railroad shares and not to another group of stocks. In making charts, one should keep a graphic for every active issue listed on the board, because every stock has its own individuality. The individual stock, while likely to move in unison with the group to which it belongs, does not always do so. It may have a little movement all its own, either in the same direction as those of its kind, but more accentuated, or in the opposite direction. The individual chart will show this peculiarity while the composite chart may not indicate it. These individual or single charts may be kept in a book, say 5½ by 7½ inches, containing about 200 blank pages. Such a book will suffice for a graphic record of stocks, grain, cotton, to cover a period of about six months. Some persons prefer a loose-leaf record. The spaces between the lines on the pages of the book may represent a point in stocks and a cent in cereals. For use in cotton fluctuations, the spaces between the lines may represent 5 points (equivalent to ¼ point in stocks), since 20 points ($1 a bale) in cotton corresponds with one point in stocks and grain. This arrangement will give ¼ divisions instead ⅛, as in stocks and cereals.

In making up a chart of daily fluctuations, start at the opening price, then follow above or below to obtain the high and low immediately succeeding the opening price, then the fluctuations of ½ point or more above or below the day's preceding high or low and the final price for the day. Note just above each day's fluctuations the date of the month, and if the stock is ex-dividend, mark it so with the amount, on the date it was ex-dividend. In applying Rule 3, it is necessary to have a record of the ex-dividend disbursements and the date and amount of same. (See ex-dividend diagram under Rule 3).

Puts and Calls

These are contracts or privileges sold whereby the seller of the privilege undertakes, in the case of a Put, to pay a set price for a given number of shares or a given quantity of commodities within a stipulated time, and in the case of a "Call" a similar contract is made to deliver the shares or commodities agreed upon at a set price. The Call names a price above the current price; the Put below the prevailing price—the distance depending upon the activity of the stock or commodity, its technical position and the period covered by the privilege. A privilege for a day only would be made closer to the market than one for a week or longer, so one for a month would be farther away and would cost more than one for a day or a week. At any time during the life of the privilege, the purchaser thereof may notify the seller of the privilege that he desires to close the contract. Of course, until the Call price has been reached, the privilege has only a contingent value, but the moment the price is touched, the buyer may have his privilege executed by the seller. In the case of a Call, the higher the stock or commodity rises above the call price, the larger the indicated profit. So the lower the stock or commodity declines below the Put price, the greater the indicated profit. Some of the sellers of Puts and Calls, where a profit is indicated, settle with the buyers on the difference between the Put or Call price and the indicated price on the board when the buyer "Puts" to or "Calls" on the seller. When a stock or commodity has been "called" and a profit indicated, it is only a paper profit and a sale is in order to convert it into an actual or cash profit. So in the case of a Put profit, a purchase of the stock or commodity is necessary in order to convert it into cash.

On the Chicago Board of Trade, Puts and Calls are designated as Insurances or Bids and Offers. Persons with small capital, or those who know little of the speculative game, are inclined to buy Puts and Calls. I once talked with a Put and Call dealer about the Put and Call "game." He told me it was much like taking candy from a baby. He knew from experience.

Buying Puts and Calls good for a day or a week is usually a losing venture, whether they be bought from a "fly-by-night" irresponsible fellow or from those who have them guaranteed by a reputable broker. My advice has always been—DON'T. There are occasions, however, when one may buy a privilege or option with some prospect of a profit after a substantial advance or decline. These occasions are in an over extended bull movement or after an extended decline, and at the moment when everybody is bearish. A Put in the first instance and a Call in the second, good for 30 days will generally bring profits. It is well to beware of a certain class of Put and Call "sharks," who advertise in such style as to fire the imagination of the unwary victim. Puts and Calls obtained through the mail pay about 99 per cent profit—to the sellers of these privileges.

Futures

Trading in cereals, Cotton, Sugar, Coffee, Pork, Lard, Ribs, etc., is generally on margin and for future delivery, i. e., to be delivered before the end of the future option month named in the contract. For example: A buys Wheat in June to be delivered in September (called September Wheat) or December or May Wheat to be delivered in December and May, respectively. He must sell it before the future month named in the purchase contract expires. He may sell it on the same day he bought, or on any subsequent day up to the last day of the month preceding the one named in the option. So if he sells (short) say December Wheat, he must deliver it not later than November 30th. This he does by buying (covering) the number of bushels he sold short. So, if he sells Cotton short in October to be delivered in December, January, March or May, he must deliver it (by buying) on or before the expiration of the month preceding the one named in the contract. He may, however, buy in (cover) on the same day he sells (short) or at any time before the first day of the option month named in the contract. This is done by "buying it in" or "covering" the short sale. Every transaction requires two operations—buying and selling or selling (short) and buying (to deliver what was sold short). One may hold a long trade in any future through the month named in the contract, but he will in such a case be required to pay elevator or warehouse charges on such holdings. These charges average about one cent a bushel per month. It is always advisable to close out long trades before the last day of the month preceding the one named in the option, as for example, on or before November 30 in a December option. Short sales must be closed out before the first day of the option month, since on the first day of the option month the commodity becomes "cash stuff." It is then referred to as cash wheat, cash corn, spot cotton, etc.

What to Guard Against in Making Commitments

Never "plunge" unless you are a skilled speculator. Plunging is hazardous. Never "pyramid"—that is, buy and accept small profits, then buy again, using the profits of the preceding trades as part of the original capital, then placing Stop Loss orders just under buying points and just over short sales points. This plan is extremely hazardous, since the reaction or rally is liable to reach the Stops. Such a plan of action is like building a pyramid with the apex of the pyramid reversed. Caution should be exercised in buying after a stock or commodity has made a spectacular perpendicular rise, because a sudden sharp and substantial reaction is in order. The same rule applies to a downward movement of like character. An old Homeric maxim reads something like this: "Never pursue your enemy too far, lest he in desperation turn on you." This old maxim still holds good. Another costly mistake a speculator sometimes makes is in taking a risk of suffering large losses. He makes a commitment and then is inclined to hold, on the theory that it will "come back" and show him a profit. One should never be guilty of making such a mistake. A Stop Loss should always be placed behind every trade and if properly placed a reverse commitment made at that point. By such action the speculator limits his losses and recoups on the reverse operation; whereas, when he continues to hold a stock against the trend, he is liable to suffer severe losses. Perhaps more unskilled speculators are wrecked financially through holding on and putting up margins indefinitely than in any other way. It is sometimes hard for a speculator to accept a small loss, but whatever is hard to do marketwise is usually the right thing, and whatever is easy is generally the wrong thing to do. Many inexperienced speculators buy stocks immediately preceding the ex-dividend date, hoping thereby to get both a speculative profit and the dividend. This is a mistaken theory, because when a stock is ex-dividend the amount of the dividend is taken off the price of the stock, and while in rare cases the dividend is soon regained in a bull market, yet in most instances such is not the case. So it is well never to buy a stock merely in order to obtain the dividend disbursement.

The Ticker

This instrument records on a strip of paper called the tape, the transactions being made on the floor of the Exchange. The stock ticker registers the name of the stock, the number of shares and the price of the same immediately following the transaction on the floor of the Exchange. The ticker is to the market what the barometer is to the weather. Both forecast approaching changes. This little instrument gives the signals or signs that the laws of market movements are in operation and are about to develop into a minor or major movement. The makers of the markets (insiders or manipulators) are not given to telling the "outsiders" what they are actually doing marketwise. Their actions—and actions speak louder than words—are registered on the tape through the Ticker, so he who is able to read the language which this instrument uses, is prepared to anticipate the movement likely to follow.

Signs and Symptoms

It is a well known fact that *Nature* has a way of giving *signs, symptoms or warnings* of the approaching operations of her laws, as for instance: *indications of coming rains, storms* or other meteorological *disturbances;* signs that precede the advent of *Spring* and other seasons; the symptoms that warn men of threatened physical or mental *disorder.* So, in the markets, a stock or commodity never makes a decided movement without first giving some sign before the execution of such a movement. Unfortunately, few persons are able to discern these signs and so are unprepared to benefit through them.

All men have neither the time nor the inclination to investigate or discover the *various phenomena of Nature,* so they are willing to follow the rules or directions laid down by those who have such inclinations, and who are acknowledged authorities in their special lines of effort. Thus it is the physician is able to diagnose an ailment or malady from given symptoms or signs observable in the patient.

The experienced navigator can predict coming changes in the weather by observing the clouds and from the appearance of the sun as it rises above or descends below the horizon. He has an instrument on board his ship that is unerring in its predictions of coming meteorological changes, so when in doubt as to his "weather eye," he consults this instrument—the *Barometer.*

Now the ticker (or the tape) is to the skilled market observer or operator what the barometer is to the experienced navigator.

Experience an Expensive Teacher

The science of speculation may be learned or mastered through experience and close observation, but only after a long, tedious and heart-breaking apprenticeship; besides, such methods are exceedingly expensive. Even the person who possesses special aptitude for the game requires years of experience to "catch on," while the average person might not be able to learn more than the rudimentary principles or laws of movements in a life time. All of this personal investigation and experience may be obviated by making use of what I offer in this book.

Through many years of experience, and by close observation I have discovered the *laws of market movements.* These market laws do not change. They work out today just as they did twenty or more years ago, so I feel safe in saying: *"It's the same old game, played in the same old way."* It is no small job to coax NATURE to give up her *secrets.* I found that she reluctantly released the secrets that I wormed from her. Every law of market movements that I have discovered has been tested scores of times before it was accepted, and if it did not repeat itself at least 9 *times in* 10, it was rejected. After being convinced through such tests that I had discovered the laws for the various phases of market movements, I formulated RULES or directions for acting in harmony with them. I then set to work to ascertain a method for action in cases of an exception to any Rule and after diligent efforts discovered a method for recouping losses that might ensue through an exception to the *Rules;* so no matter what phase of movements may be encountered there is a *Rule* furnished herein that applies and fits the change.

VII
RULES

Diagrams
Charts

Everything requiring skill that is done or performed correctly or rightly by man is in accordance with Rules formulated to act in harmony with natural laws. The Rules set forth herein for the guidance of speculators and investors are in harmony with the laws governing in market fluctuations or movements. The Rules given in this work cover about every phase of market movements. Where one Rule leaves off another comes in to cover the next movement. They interlock. To every phase of the markets' movements there is a Rule that applies to meet the requirements of the situation. Following are the Rules with explanations for their application.

No. 1—Opening Rule

This Rule determines at the opening of the market whether the market or a particular stock or a commodity is a purchase or a sale for that day. It is of especial value in cases when a particular stock or commodity closes at the top after a substantial advance or at the bottom of a substantial decline.

Opening Rule for Determining Whether the Market is a Purchase or a Sale, etc.

There are but two positions or stations in the stock or commodity markets from which to form accurate estimates as to the next probable moves, viz:

First: When the stocks or commodities close at the top.

Second: When the stocks or commodities close at the bottom.

For the purpose of elucidating this rule, we shall confine our directions and explanations to the stock market.

If the active list of stocks closes mixed or irregular, i. e.—some at a decline from the best prices of the day and others at an advance from the lowest of the day, there is no known method by which an estimate may be made as to the next probable move, but the chances are, if the list opens in the same manner as it closed, viz:—mixed or irregular, the market will be a sale on a moderate advance from the initial opening or a purchase on a moderate decline from the opening prices. Such a market movement usually ends at about the same level as the preceding day's closing prices.

The object in closing the market at the top and at the bottom from time to time is to form an estimate of its relative strength or weakness.

A—SELL.—If the market closes at the top, and the next morning's opening discloses shading in prices all along the line and in some issues no improvement in prices, such a market is a sale for profits in proportion to the advance made from the bottom of the last preceding recession, and if such advance has been of two days or so duration, the market will be a sale on all rallies for the entire day and close at the bottom.

It is not necessary that every active stock shall show shading or "no better" on such an opening. Two-thirds of the active list will serve for the purpose, and one-half will be sufficient on which to sell the market on an advance from its opening.

B—BUYS.—If the market closes at the bottom, and the next morning's opening evidences improvement in prices all along the line and in some shares "no worse" in prices, such a market is a purchase for profits proportioned to the decline from the top of the last preceding advance or rally, and if such decline has been of two days or so duration, the market will be a purchase on dips during the entire day, with chances of a top closing. It is not necessary that every active stock shall show improvement or "no worse" on such an opening. Two-thirds of the active lists will serve for the purpose—and even one-half will suffice for the purpose of a purchase on recession from the opening prices.

Examples to illustrate the foregoing section of this rule.

SELL.—The market closes at the top.—S. P. at 120—it's top price. The next morning's opening shows shading, etc., as above outlined. S. P. opens at 120—or 119⅞. Such an opening indicates weakness and should be counted "down." Had it opened at 120⅛ or better, it would be counted "up."

BUY.—The market closes at the bottom. S. P. closes at 118½—the bottom. The next morning's opening indicates improvement, etc., as above explained. S. P. opens at 118½ or 118⅝, or better. Such an opening evidences strength and should be counted "up." Had it opened at 118⅜ or "worse," it would be counted "down." In counting at opening after a top close, count as weak or "down" those stocks that show shading or are "no better" than the close on the preceding day.

In counting at opening after a bottom closing, count as strong or "up" those stocks that show improvement or "no worse" than the preceding day's closing.

In the case of a "top" closing—what stocks should be sold if the next morning's opening discloses shading, etc.?

SELL.—ANSWER: Those that have been the most active and have enjoyed the greatest advance—provided these closed at the top and show shading, etc., in the morning's opening.

BUY.—In the case of a bottom closing—what stocks should be bought if the next morning's opening discloses improvement, etc.?

ANSWER: Those that have been the most active and have suffered the greatest decline—provided these closed at the bottom and show improvement, etc. When the market closes at the top or at the bottom, the chances are it will continue next morning in the direction aimed at the close.

BUY.—If the market opens slightly better than its top close, the chances are it will advance further, and will be a purchase on the first recession for that point in the advance where animation or buoyancy is in evidence. Here is the point at which to take profits—since there is no other known way by which to estimate the extent of such advance, and since it may mark the culmination point until after a reaction—await a recession commensurate with the advance made from the bottom of the last previous reaction, before purchasing, or a "sign" at the opening.

SELL.—If the market opens slightly "worse" than its bottom close, the chances are it will decline further, and will be a sale on the first rally for that point in the decline where animation or demorilization is in evidence. Here is the point at which to take profits, since there is no other known way by which to gauge the extent of such decline, and it may be the culmination point until after a rally. So await an uplift proportioned to the decline from the top of the last previous, or a "sign" at the opening before selling short.

When stocks open wide—either up or down—caution should be exercised in making commitments. Such openings are to be viewed with suspicion. They are generally followed by a reverse movement in the market. Quick profits should always be accepted.

In counting stocks "up" and "down" it must be borne in mind that all stocks have not the same value as "counters," but their value is in proportion to their activity and volume of transactions.

For the purpose of "counting," a list of about twenty active stocks should be kept and used. The movements of these from day to day should be noted. As the active ones become dormant, substitute with *new* active issues.

Deal in "FEATURES" to the exclusion of all other issues.

NOTE—Any person who circulates copies of this rule will be prosecuted in accordance with the provision of the U. S. Statutes.

Explanation of Opening Rule

(Rule 1)

This Rule is intended primarily for day to day movements in stocks and commodities. When the fluctuations are narrow then only members of Exchanges can make use of it for day to day profitable results because they pay no commission on commitments. When, however, the fluctuations run to a couple of points or more daily, then the outsider can use the Rule to advantage. When the market has a decided trend upward and the close is at the top—followed by shading in the morning as referred to in Paragraph marked A, the unskilled operator will accept long profits and await a recession to the technical adjustment point, then buy for another upward or forward movement. These suggestions apply equally to a decided downward movement (bear market) only the operation is reversed as in Paragraph marked B. Where, however, the advance has extended over a period of a couple of days and there has been a substantial advance from the last technical adjustment or buying point, then the novice may safely follow the directions given in Paragraph A—sell short on signs of shading. In a similar condition he also may buy under Paragraph B when a "no worse" sign is in evidence. Sometimes under Paragraph A after the sign is given to sell—a stock or commodity advances. So under Paragraph marked B after the sign is given to buy—a stock or commodity—declines. In such cases we sell on advances in the first instance and buy on the dips or recessions in the second. When a stock or commodity closes at the top of a rally and shows no higher the next morning, it is treated as in the case where it closes at the actual top (see Paragraph A). So also when a stock or commodity closes at the bottom of a dip and opens no lower next morning, then such opening is to be treated as in the case of an actual bottom close (see Paragraph B). These instructions under the above paragraph are for skilled operators only. In order to apply this Rule to the best advantage, it is well to keep a record of the fluctuations from the close to the end of the day. The opening; the change after the opening; every half point change or more above the high or below the low after the opening, and the closing price, to the close and the change next to the close. For example: Steel Com. closed yesterday at 90, the top. Opened 89⅞ then to 88⅝, 89⅜, 88⅛, bottom. The fluctuations between 88⅞ and 89¾ are negligible because, first—the full fluctuation was less than a full point and second—it did not overtop 89⅞, but the one to below 88⅝ is significant. The next morning, it opens 88⅛, dips to 87⅝, then 88¾, 88, 89¾. The opening price would be noted, then 87⅝, 88¾, but not necessarily 88, because it did not decline a full point, or below 87⅝. The last quotation being the top for the day, we may dismiss all intermediate movements between 87⅝ and 89¾, since this Rule is intended to apply only in top and bottom closes. A reference to the daily newspapers' stock and commodity quotations will usually suffice for the purposes of applying Rule One.

For exact changes during the day, consult the official list kept on file in all broker's offices.

If at any time you are inclined to imagine the Rule does not work out or that the movement is an exception to the Rule, just take time to examine into the application of the Rule in such market movements. The chances are you will find that the seat of the trouble is in the application of the Rule itself. If at any time your opinion conflicts with the directions under the Rule, better follow the Rule rather than your opinion, since opinions are often misleading and when followed often lead to disastrous results. Study the Rule carefully and thoroughly, the more you do so, the more of merit you will find in it. It is essential to be accurate in the use of fractions. Of all the fractions, the ⅛ is the most important under this and other Rules herein. I suggest that you use this Rule in connection with past markets for the purpose of familiarizing yourself with the practical application of the Rule. These will serve quite as well for the purpose as will future ones. Mistakes carry their penalties in this business as well as in all other lines of activities, so AVOID mistakes and FOLLOW the Rule.

P. S. A severe penalty attaches for circulating copies of Rules protected by Copyright.

Rule 2

(Copyright, 1909, by W. C. Moore)

When a stock reaches a certain price beyond the point where it has been on the current movement, and recedes or advances from such high or low point—three points, without having practically reached such high or low the second time after one point or more reaction, it is a purchase or sale for one point or more profit; and if conditions have not changed in the general situation in the meantime, the chances are such stock will advance or decline to practically the high or low point on the first movement.

At the point where such stock is a purchase or sale, in accordance with the three-point rule, the general list will act in sympathy, *i. e.*, be a purchase or sale as in case of the special stock.

In case of an advance in market followed by a recession, the last in point of time to advance and make the three-point recession under the rule, is the safest to purchase. Such movement of this particular stock usually marks the turning point in the whole market for a material advance. This rule reversed applies to a falling market.

Suppose the market is an advancing one, and Atchison has touched 99—a price beyond that heretofore made in the current movement; now a reaction sets in, and the whole list recedes. Atch. has been 99, 98½, 98¾, 98¼, 97½, 98¼, 97, 97½, 96. It is a purchase at 96. Suppose it had been 99, then 98, then 99, 98⅞ or 99⅛, then down to 96; such a movement would not come under the three-point rule. If the trend be downward, then the same rule reversed, would apply, and the chances are the list would turn when this particular stock reached three points upwards from low.

NOW, another illustration of the Rule, and this time on a downward trend. A. R. has declined with the others and is the last one in the list to reach its low, say 90. It touches low but once, and from that point reacts, thus: 90, 90½, 91, 90¾, 91½, 91, 92, 91½, 93. This last figure is the selling point, and the chances are the whole market is a sale when A. R. reaches 93. If it goes to 90, then 91, 90 or 90⅛ or 89⅞, then 93, such a move would not be governed by the three-point rule, because it has reached the low the second time. In stocks like Rdg., U. P., S. P., St. P. and some other high-priced issues, the advance or decline sometimes exceeds three points.

On much animation I have seen them make 4 to 4½ points reaction under the three-point rule; but they are safe at three points. In stocks selling at about 150, it is well to give these high priced ones a little latitude under the rule, *i. e.*, go beyond three points if there be unusual animation in the market.

Keep a list of the active stocks, and mark every change of one-half point in their advance or decline. This plan will enable you to keep tab on the stocks coming under the three-point rule.

Note—This Rule, like Rule 3, was formulated at a time when movements in stocks and commodities were more conservative than in 1914-20. So, while it is still applicable to stocks that move over a comparatively narrow range, yet it is not so in all movements in all stocks or in all commodities. The Rule does not apply to erratic or volatile issues, nor to Wheat, Corn and Cotton in excited movements. The Rule applies particularly to those issues that move in a conservative way. It applies to Standard Rail Shares and to Industrials, Mining Stocks and other seasoned issues with prices below 125.

Rule 3

(Copyright, 1909, by W. C. Moore)

The market advances and recedes by waves or stages.

When it advances beyond the previous high wave, or declines below the previous receding wave, the chances are it will average at least two points further than such previous high or low point, so we have this law, which applies with equal force to a special or particular stock, thus the *Rule.* When a stock has established a certain high or low point in its movement the chances are, if the succeeding movement or wave carries it beyond or below such preceding high or low—to the extent of one-half point, such stock is a purchase or sale as the movement indicates—on the first reaction, for that point in the advance or decline equal to two points beyond or below the preceding high or low.

If the trend of the general market is favorable to such movement in the special stock—then only a moderate reaction suffices for the purpose of buying or selling the special stock for the two points advance or decline before mentioned. When such special stock becomes very active, and the general market is in a favorable condition to sympathize—the reaction may not materialize but the stock continue the move to the two points stage and even further. It is, however, the safer plan to allow a reaction in the stock before making a commitment.

If the special stock gives the "sign" for the two points advance or decline, and the market at the time is in an exhausted condition by reason of a continuous advance or a continuous or material decline, more than one-half point or so reaction should be allowed the special stock before making a commitment. For example: Suppose the market had enjoyed a continuous and substantial advance for two or more days—and exhibited animation or buoyancy on the top (which usually is indication of a general reaction to follow), at the time when the special stock gives the sign it is then the safer plan to wait for a substantial recession in the market before purchasing such special stock. Should such recession end in a quick, violent dip throughout the general list—then the special stock is the one to purchase. Same rule *reversed* applies to a falling market. In most cases the two points advance or decline aforesaid are made on the day that the "sign" is in evidence, but in cases of an exhausted market heretofore mentioned—one or more days may elapse before conditions are favorable to complete the move. Of course, if general conditions change materially since the "sign" was given it is unreasonable to expect the Rule to apply. If conditions remain practically as they were when the sign was given, the chances are the special stock will act in accordance with the Rule.

In acting under the Rule, we must not confound a preceding move with a present or continuous move. To illustrate: Atch. is moving up—it indicates 92½, 91¾, 93, 92, 92½, 92, 92½, 93, etc. Now, the first 93 after 92½ would not be a half point under the Rule, since it is a continuous move. Had it made 92½ on another move a week or a month or months before—and on the present move touched 93—then the two-point rule would apply. Here is another illustration where it would apply, although apparently the move is continuous, viz.: Atch. 90, 92, 90½, 92, 90, 92½, 92, 94 or 95. The first move concluded when Atch. reached 92 and no more the second time. The next wave carried it beyond the strength or force of the former move, so the succeeding one-half point advance is a "new move" and indicates an advance to 94.

How to Apply Rule 3 After a Stock Becomes Ex-Dividend

In applying Rule 3, ex-dividend must be taken into account. In reckoning the advance of one-half point beyond a former high preceding the date when a stock becomes ex-dividend, the amount of the ex-dividend must be subtracted from its high before the ex-dividend date; or added to the price of the stock after it becomes ex-dividend. In either case, when so treated, they are equivalents under the Rule. In the first instance, equivalents *before* ex-dividend, and in the second, equivalents *after* ex-dividend. When those equivalents have been determined, then the Rule for one-half point beyond applies.

So, in order to determine the equivalents after ex-dividend in a declining or downward movement, we subtract from the low price preceding ex-dividend the amount of the dividend, *i. e.*, reduce its price equal to the dividend rate; or increase the price of the stock to the extent of the dividend rate after it becomes ex-dividend. Either method determines the equivalents for before and for after ex-dividend.

The following Diagram illustrates the foregoing explanation:

A. Ex-dividend, 1½%, January 20th. Now we have on January 22d, 7½. This is equivalent to 9 before ex-dividend (adding 1½), or by subtracting

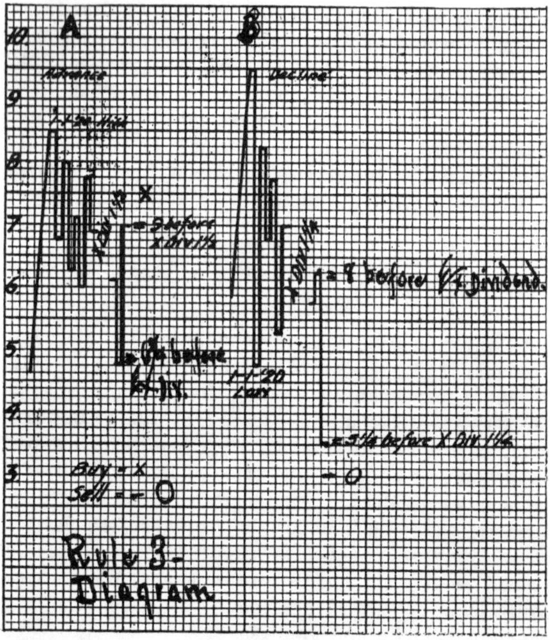

1½ from 9 we have 7½, its equivalent after ex-dividend. So, we have under the Rule, the buying point, 8 (X).

B. Ex-dividend, 1¼%, January 10th. We have here 4, which is equivalent to 5¼ before ex-dividend (adding 1¼). Now, subtracting 1¼ from 5¼ we have 4, the equivalent of low before ex-dividend, and the selling point, 3½ (O), under Rule 3. The ex-dividend is to be taken into account under Rule 3 for about three weeks or so after the ex-dividend date.

The foregoing Rule was formulated at a time when movements were more normal or conservative than after the war period set in. So the Rule should be construed accordingly. The movements beyond previous tops and bottoms under the Rule should be considered as acting in conjunction with the Swing Rule instead of limiting them to the conservative *two* points further advance or decline named in the Rule. (See Swing Rule.)

The "older" the previous tops or bottoms, the better under Rule 3. That is to say, the longer the time that elapses between the former highs or lows and the ones being acted on under the Rule, the better the results are likely to be. This is the most important Rule of any in the series. It is to the others what the Sun is to the solar system. You will find the half point advances and declines play a very important part in other Rules herein and in all phases of market movement, so it is important that you study this Rule carefully and thoroughly to get it indelibly impressed upon your mind for immediate application when an occasion presents itself.

Special Directions When Applying Rule 3

A. If the half point advance beyond the former top or the decline below the former bottom be slowly made, then in such a case you would better not wait for a reaction in the first instance or a rally in the second, but buy immediately at the fractional advance and sell at the fractional recession under the Rule. If, however, the fractional advance or decline beyond highs or lows be rapid, then you will buy on the first reaction (dip) and sell on the first rally of a point or so, depending upon how far the advance or decline has extended beyond the former top or the former bottom, then hold your commitment over until the next day, when profits may be accepted. The Swing Rule will guide you as to the probable extent of the advance or the decline beyond the former top or bottom. Of course, in case of a commitment being made on a "Buy on Stop" order, or on a "Sell on Stop" order, such an order becomes effective and is executed immediately after the price named in the order is reached, so the differentiation in fast and slow movements beyond previous tops or bottoms could not be exercised. A "Buy on Stop" or a "Sell on Stop" may be given the broker in expectation that a named stock or a named commodity may reach the price at which it would be a purchase or a sale under the Rule. This order may be a "K. G. C." This same form of order should be used in case an exception to Rule 3 develops, and Rule 4 applies. (Consult order forms on another page.)

Rule 4

How to Act When the Movement Under Rule 3 Proves an Exception to Said Rule

When a stock or commodity is bought under Rule 3 and fails to respond in accordance with said Rule, then the following directions apply:

If, after the stock or commodity reaches the buying point under the Rule, then declines straight downward a full point or more up to 2½ points (not 3 straight points, since the latter movement would come under Rule 2), then rallies a full point or more, but not sufficient to reach one-half point above the initial buying point under the Rule, then declines one-half point below the preceding decline from the top—one full point or more up to 2½ points' decline, you will stop loss on the long trade at the one-half point lower than the first full point or more recession from the top and reverse the commitment at that *point or price*, *i. e.*, sell short double the number of shares that were bought for the initial advance, and hold the short sale for a profit equal to the loss sustained in such first purchase. The object in thus selling short being to recoup only the losses incurred through the exception to the Rule.

These same instructions apply to a declining market where the operator is selling short under the Rule—with this difference, that the operation is reversed. The principles, however, are identical.

See examples in graphic chart below, explaining the foregoing.

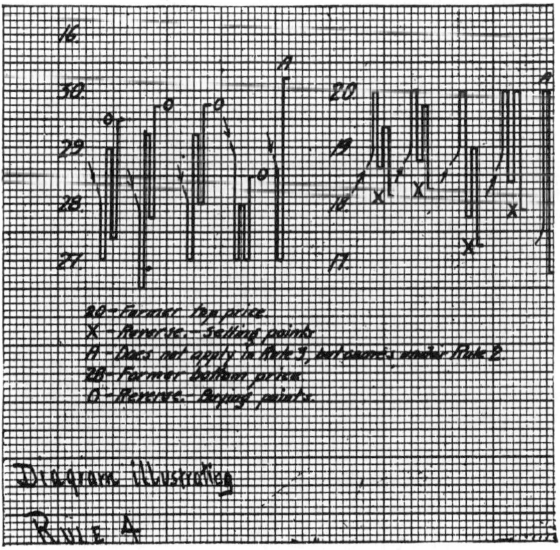

Rule 6

A Rule for Rapid Movements

This Rule is for determining the reaction points at which to sell on rapid movements—near the top and when to buy at or near the bottom of such movements.

It is the best of all the Rules for quick profits. It is THE Rule for the man who sits close to the board or ticker when such movements are in action.

When a stock, grain or cotton has made a substantial advance and such advance is supplemented by a quick further run upward and this is followed by a reaction of a point or more, then is lifted a point or more, but to a price not beyond the preceding high point, then reacts one-half point below the preceding point of reaction from the high point, the stock, grain or cotton is a sale at such point or price—that is, one-half point below the preceding reaction price. So, if long of such a stock or commodity, a Stop Loss should be placed at the half point below, and the trade be reversed at such half point below. This same Rule

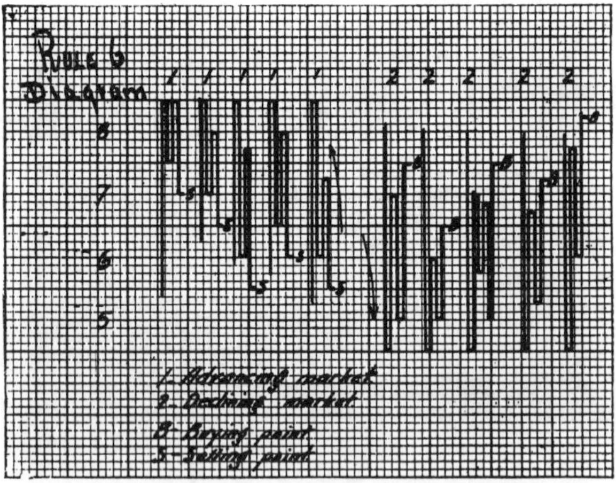

applies in a declining market, only the operation is reversed. When such long or short trades are made on a reverse movement, quick profits should be taken, and if not taken and the stock or commodity continues in the direction of its major movement (up or down) the trade should be again reversed at a price one-half point beyond the extreme high on an upward movement, and one-half below on a downward movement.

One full dollar counts as a point in stocks; one full cent as a point in grain, and twenty points in cotton are counted equivalent to a dollar in stocks and a cent in grain, under this Rule.

The following graphic chart will serve to illustrate the foregoing Rule. Between heavy lines are full points.

Rule 7

Technical Adjustments

This Rule is for determining adjustments, *i. e.*, the extent of minor rallies and reactions in major movements. It gives the buying and selling points in following the trend. The minor movements which go to make what are termed technical adjustments are natural and in obedience to the laws of market movements in general. They may be likened to what occurs when a rubber ball is dropped from various heights to the floor or ground—a rebound or "rally" ensues after it touches the point of resistance, and this rally or rebound will be proportionate to the distance of the fall of the ball. The rallies that make the technical adjustments are usually caused by covering (buying in) short trades made at a higher price in a declining market and by reactions on profit taking on an advancing movement. These reactions and rallies are proportionate in extent to the advances and the declines before they set in to make the technical adjustment.

In an advancing market as in a declining one, when movements are orderly, rallies and reactions in the minor movements are practically and proportionately the same as in the major ones, *i. e.*, the law works the same in both movements. These minor movements may be likened to the gentle waves on the surface of the sea; the major ones to the waves running high in a strong wind. In the former, they are termed technical adjustments, while in the latter they are called swings. When the minor movements or waves approach the culmination points of the major swings, these minor movements blend with the major movements and usually make a quick advance on an upward swing and similar movement (reversed) on a downward swing. When such movements are in evidence, a reverse movement or trend may be anticipated. Reactions on an upward movement are usually equal to about one-half the advance from the bottom of the preceding reaction point. Rallies on a declining movement are usually equal to about one-half the decline from the top of the preceding rally.

In both advancing and declining swings, the high and low are approximately reached a second time after a reaction or rally. See Diagram No. 7.

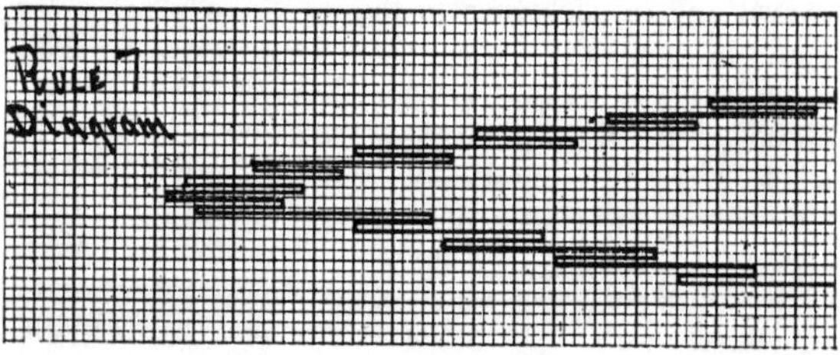

Rule 8

When the market or a particular stock or commodity opens upward on two successive days after a preceding downward opening, the chances are for a top close on such second day's opening. So, when the market or a particular stock or commodity opens down two successive days, the chances are for a bottom close on such second day. In either case, a third successive day of like opening does not apply.

Modification of Rule 8

If, however, in such second day's opening upward or downward, the movement in the direction thus indicated at the opening of the market is made early in the day, it is not so likely to close at the top or at the bottom, because the movement due is already made. Only in the case where the indicated movement is postponed until late in the day, may we expect the top or bottom close under this Rule.

Diagram No. 8 illustrates the application of the Rule.

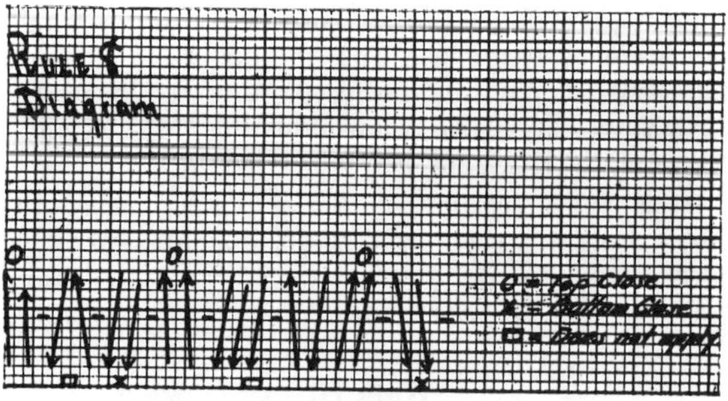

Rule 9

A Rule for making commitments near the close of the market. This is a splendid Rule for making quick profits on the following day. When a stock or commodity begins to move upward into new ground, *i. e.*, beyond its recent or former high, the chances are it will extend its movement still further on the following day, so may be bought near the close of the market. If, however, such stock or commodity closes at the top and at the opening of the market next morning opens no higher than the closing price of the previous day, then close out the commitment "at the market" and sell this stock or commodity short "at the market" at or near the price at which it closed on the previous day.

This same Rule applies in the case of a stock or commodity closing at the bottom. In this case, of course, the stock or commodity should be sold short for an anticipated profit on the following day. If, however, the stock or commodity sold short opens next morning at a price no lower than the bottom closing price of the day previous, cover (buy in) such short trade and then go long (buy) such stock or commodity for an anticipated advance instead of the decline expected when the short trade was made at or near the close on the preceding day. When trades are made in accordance with the directions given in this Rule, they are at the inception of the movement anticipated, so should show profits in nine commitments out of a possible ten.

Note—When commitments are made under the Rules herein, such commitments should be carried over to the following day except where the Rules apply to one-day movements.

Rule 10

Stop Loss Rule

This Rule directs at what price a "Stop Loss" should be placed on both a long and a short commitment. Every trade should be protected by a Stop—and if the Stop is scientifically placed, a reverse trade should be made at such Stop Loss price.

A Stop Loss order should be placed one-half point beyond the recent high or low of a current movement, following a full point rally or dip; and a reverse commitment should be made at such Stop Loss point for profits at least sufficient to recoup the loss on the initial trade and perhaps more—depending upon the intensity of the reverse movement.

Diagram No. 10 illustrates the Rule.

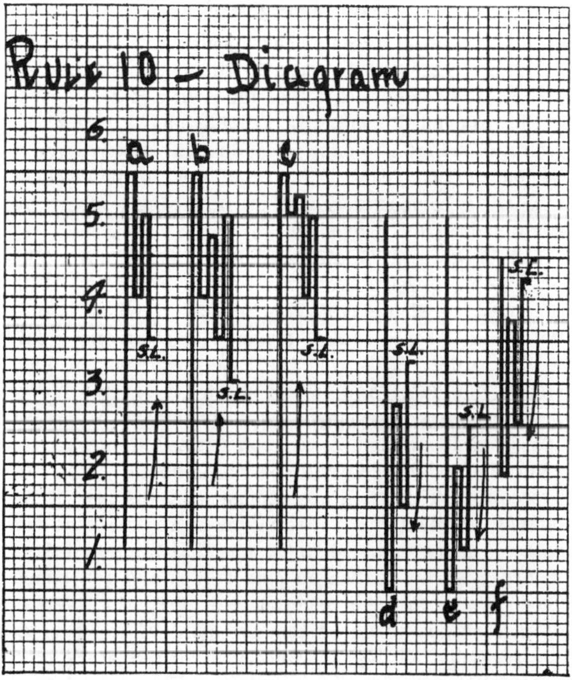

A B C indicate initial purchases on an upward movement.

C D E indicate initial sales on a downward movement.

S L indicate Stop Loss and reverse commitment points.

Rule 5
The Swing Rule

This combined graphic chart of about 25 Industrials as shown herein will serve to illustrate the law of swings and the application of the Swing Rule.

The appended composite graphic chart shows the average swings of about 25 Industrial stocks over a period of two years. The same law of movements applies in composite groups as in a single stock; in grain, cotton and provisions.

Let us go over it and see how it works out. The first swing upward from the low in February, 1919, extended to about 119½ in November, when it culminated. That is to say, reached its peak and a fall was in order. This was the time to go out of long stock (liquidate) and to sell short. A reverse movement followed carrying stocks downward to about 101½, or 18 points. A rebound carried it upward to about 110, which you will observe is about ½ the fall preceding. This is in accordance with the law of rebounds or reactions. We may now assume that the rebound has exhausted itself and that another fall is in order, so we realize on long trades and sell short. The chances are the reaction will carry the average of prices back to about the low point of the preceding recession (101½) because generally a stock or a commodity reaches a high or low point a second time after a reaction or a rally or rebound, provided conditions have not changed materially in the meantime. Anyway, we shall act on this assumption and operate accordingly, and if the decline extends to 99½ (Rule 3) we will sell again for a decline to a point as much lower than 101½ as the distance between 119½ and 101½ (18 points) or to 83½. This is as far as we are able to forecast at this juncture. The decline reached about 89½ (20½ points), then rebounded.

After 20 points advance or decline of a stock or commodity, we may anticipate a reverse movement of about ½ of the entire major movement. In this case the major decline from 119½ to 89½ is 30 points; ½ backward equals 15 points; 15 plus 89½ equals 104½. We may now begin to anticipate a reverse or downward swing to at least the former low point (89½) and perhaps to the price indicated above (83½). Now that the decline has passed 89½ we are justified in forecasting an eventual 69, i. e., as far below 89½ as the distance from 89½ to 110. (See graphic of corn when it indicated a final of 173½.) The low here is determined by identically the same method as was employed in forecasting the top of Corn. Of course, we must expect and anticipate technical adjustment on the way to the final bottom. The decline carries to about 88½, or one point lower than the preceding decline and at which price we are justified in again selling short, under Rule 3, for 83½. We get a decline to about 84½ (12 points), and a rally to about 90, or approximately ½ the preceding decline. Now declining to below 88½ indicates a further decline to 72½, i. e., as far below 88½ as the distance between 104½ and 88½ or to 72½. We get the same result after 84½ is broken, viz., as far below 84½ as the distance between 84½ and 96½ (12) or 72½, but we keep constantly in mind the 69 indicated after passing 89½.

About sixty-seven and a half was reached on a demoralized slump in the market December 22, 1920.

The graphic charts of grain and stocks shown herein will serve to illustrate the operation of the law of movements in both major movements or swings, and in minor movements for technical adjustments. The fact that the charts cover past movements, i. e., market fluctuations made last year or the year before or several years ago is immaterial for the purpose of illustrating the laws of movements, since these laws do not change. They operated 10 or 20 or more years ago the same as they do today or will do 10 or 20 years hence.

Corn Chart

Graphic Chart No. 12 applies to Corn. We will now give it attention for the purpose of familiarizing the student with the laws of movements and the Rules that apply thereto.

Starting at 165 1/2, May 17th, Extending to September 1st, 1920

Under RULE 3, we sell short on the 18th, 161⅜. Now this short sale shows a good profit. Anyway, from 165½ to 156, about 10 points, calls for a rally, so having covered somewhere near 156, and particularly so when it dipped quickly to 156. [Following a substantial advance or decline with a quick movement on an upward or a sharp decline on a downward move is a hint or signal to close out the trade.]

Now, under Rule 3 we buy at 159⅛, this being ½ point beyond the top of the rally from 156 after a set-back of a point or more. We shall close out the trade at a point about midway between 156 and 165½ in accordance with Rule 5—(Swing Rule), say at about 160½. Our next short sale will be at 155½ and this commitment should carry us down to about 146½. That is to say, as much lower than the bottom of the first downward swing (156) as the distance between the bottom (156) and the preceding top (165½) or 9½ points. Subtracting 9½ from 156, we have 146½ (consult Swing Rule). So, we cover the short trade near 146½.

Our next trade will be a purchase at 150½, following the rally from 146½ to 150, the full point recession to 149 and the advance to ½ point above 150, the top of the rally. We may buy again at 152½; again at 154½ and again at 157⅜. Now if after buying at 157⅜ and the set back to 155 had been followed by a rally of a point or more and a decline to 154½, we would under Rule 4, reverse our trade, but as it did not do so and ran up quickly to 159¾, we close out the trade at a small profit.

Our next commitment will be a short sale at ½ point below the low after 159¾ (155¼) or 154¾. A rally instead of a decline ensues extending to 157¼, followed by a recession to 153. In view of the fact that the trade had an indicated loss of about 3 points, we naturally close out this trade when it shows even a small profit, which it did near 153. We sell short again at 152½ and accept a moderate profit, because the price has had an almost perpendicular decline from 157½ to 150¼. Our next purchase under Rule 3 is at 154 on the 29th; again at 159⅞, June 2nd for a moderate profit because of a nearly straight line up from 150¼ to 161½.

Now let us pause and make a reckoning. You will observe that the rebound from 150¼ extended beyond the rebound from 146½. This means more than is revealed to the unskilled operator. It indicates that the price is likely to ascend to a point as much beyond 159¾ as the distance from the bottom of the preceding swing downward (146½) and the top of the swing upward (159¾). Subtracting 146½ from 159¾, we have 13¼ cents. We add 13¼ to 159¾ and obtain 173, so, while we shall continue to play closely as directed under Rule 3, both long and short, yet we should exercise caution on short trades, i. e., accept quick and moderate profits, since according to the Rule, 173 is likely to be reached. This we should keep in mind constantly until that price is approximately reached.

Our next commitment under Rule 3 will be 162⅜, but in view of the straight line up, i. e., advances without technical adjustments on the way, commensurate with the advance, caution should be exercised in this as in all such movements either upward or downward, extending to 10 or more cents or points. In short, wait for technical adjustments before making a commitment. The swing upward from 150¼ to 163 equals 12¾ cents, so we may expect a set-back of about ½ of that advance, or 6⅜ cents, which should carry it to about 156⅝. A reaction from 163 to 160¼ follows, with a rally that extends a cent or more, but not above 163, so we will sell at 159¾ (4th) with a Stop Loss at 163½. We sell again at 158 and again at 157¼. We will close out on a moderate profit. We do not buy at 158¾ on the 9th because the rally to 158¼ on the 8th was not from the low (155-¼). Had it been, a purchase at 158¾ would have been in order. Our next trade will be at 162¼ and at 163½ (½ point beyond the top of rebound, June 3rd). Now, since this point is passed, we again must exercise caution, because of the fact that the top of the former rebound (163) is exceeded and this means probably a still higher price. Here is another almost straight line upward of nearly 10 points, so caution is in order and we accept any quickly made profit. Our next trade is a short one at 161¼ (11th) for quick and moderate profits. The recession reaches 160¼. This being about half the distance back from 164¾ to 155¼, we cover under Rule 5 (Swing Rule). Our next commitment will be a buy at 162½ on the 11th. This carries to 165⅜. Now if we buy again at 165¾, we shall have bought at the top eighth. Right here is an appropriate place for an observation: When a stock or commodity passes the preceding high or low point rapidly, caution should be exercised under Rule 3. Usually in such cases it is best to wait for a set back before making the commitment. Nevertheless, as we are operating closely under the Rules, we shall play them as they show on the tape, so we have bought at 165¾. A reaction sets in and carries the price back to 161¾, 162⅞, 161⅝, 163, 161¼. You will observe there is no call under Rule 4, (Exception Rule) for a reverse trade, so we continue to hold our long trade at 165¾. We may buy more at 165⅜;

again at 165⅞. Now the chances are we may hold these trades for 170½. That is to say, as far beyond 165⅜ as the distance between 165⅜ and the reaction preceding 165⅜, viz., 160¼, or 5⅛ cents. Adding 5⅛ to 165⅜ we have 170½ (reached 171⅛). Now, we may buy some at 168⅞ and 169⅝ with a quick profit to follow, since the advance from 161¼ to 171¼ was without adequate reactions or technical adjustments on the way up. A technical adjustment or reaction is now in order, extending to about ½ the distance from 171¼ to 161¼ or 5 cents (reached 166¾). Now, if we did not cover our short trade near 166¾ we should under the circumstances noted above, be willing to accept a small loss, say a cent or so. Our next trade will be a buy at 171 for near 173 as indicated after passing 159¾ (June 2nd). The price reached 173½. That's near enough, but if we desire to play "hog" we hold on until Rule 3 directs us to reverse the trade which would be at 171¼. We sell again at 167½, but accept a quick profit or a small loss, because the set back from 173½ to 166⅝ was made with inadequate adjustments. There is no sign under the Rule for a reverse commitment until after 171 on the 23rd. We sell at 168⅜ on the 24th and get a moderate profit. We sell again at 166¼ (25th) and reverse our trade at 169 (26th). This trade we shall hold until our loss on the previous one is recouped. The loss was about 3½ cents. We will go out of the last (long) trade at about 172½.

Our next trade (short) is at 171. If we did not accept a small profit, there is no call to reverse under Rule 4 (Exception), so we hold our short trade. We sell again at 169½ (30th). Both trades give us profits.

We buy at 171 (July 2d). We reverse the trade at 169⅛, sell again at 165½ (½ below 166—25th); again 165, 163⅞; 162⅛, 159⅞. This swing downward is likely to carry to as far below 166 as it reached above before declining to 166, viz., 173½, minus 166, equals 7½ cents. 166 minus 7½ equals 158½ (reached 157½ —6th).

Now, since the swing downward from 173½ has extended below the one from 173½ (166), we assume that the trend is downward and should therefore exercise caution in buying, and also in taking profits on such commitments. In short, sales on rallies for the fall are safer than purchases.

Our next trade is a purchase at 160¼ (6th) and again at 162. Let us accept a quick and moderate profit. Our next trade is a short one at 157 (8th). This showed us a small profit at 155½ but we have not taken it. So we reverse the trade at 157¾ by going long. We reverse this one at 155 (sell short). It shows only a fractional profit at 154½. We will stand on the trade. We reverse again at 156⅝ (9th). At 158¼ we have a small profit but do not accept it and continue to hold. The next trade (purchase) is made at 158⅝ (10th), again at 161¼ (12th). There has been a decline of 18⅝ cents from 173⅛ and a technical adjustment rally of about one-half of this decline may be expected, *i. e.*, to 163¾ (reached 162⅞).

Now let us see how we stand on the result of the last six trades. The short trade at 157, reversed to long at 157¾ represents a loss of about 1c. The latter trade reversed at 155 indicates a loss of about 3c. This trade reversed at 156⅝ shows a loss of about 2c. and a total of about 6c. on the three trades. By closing out the three last commitments (long) at about 162 we have an indicated profit of about 5c. on the first, 3½ on the second and perhaps more on the third, or a total of about 8½c., thus more than recouping the losses on the three preceding trades.

Our next trade (short) is made at 159¾, 157¾, 155⅛, 154. Now, since there is shown a decline of over 10 points from 162⅞, we shall take profits around

152. We buy at 54⅜ on 15th. We reverse again (short) at 151 and again at 148¼ and close out on a quick dip, say about 147½ or 148 for profits enough to recoup our losses on purchase at 154⅜, which just about recouped our losses.

Our next trade will be long at 150 (16th). We accept a fractional profit because of uncertain narrow movements. Our next trade (19th) at 151½. Accept another small profit. Next trade at 149¾ short, and accept quick moderate profits. Next trade long, 153¼ (22d). Accept moderate profit, because rally to 155 from 147 is about one-half of decline from 162⅞ to 147. Now short at 152 (24th). Sell again at 146½ (see 16th and 17th). This swing should extend to about 14⅞c. below 147, *i. e.*, the distance between 162⅞ and 147, or to about 131⅛. Sell at 145⅛; again at 140½ (27th), and cover on quick, sharp dip. Buy at 142¾ and accept a moderate profit (29th). Next trade—sell 139⅞ (30th); again 138½; 136¼ (31st). It seems by its actions to have declined far enough—about 40c. from top. Our next purchase is at 136. Now, if this is the bottom of the major swing, then the rebound should extend to one-half of the decline from 173½, or to 153⅝.

From what has been shown in the movements from 173½ to 133¾ should suffice to explain how the minor movements should be played. We have applied the Rule almost mechanically, disregarding judgment. This has been done in order to demonstrate how the Rule works, and at the same time to teach the reader the finer points of the speculative game. Of course, the speculator of experience would not attempt to play the game so mechanically as carried out in this explanatory exercise. Let us see about what he would have done:

First trade—Short at 161¾ (Rule 3).
Second trade—Short at 155½ (Rule 3).
Third trade—Long at 150½ (Rule 6).

Fourth trade—Long at 154½ (Rule 3), closing out at about 156, rebound of about one-half of decline preceding downward swing.

Fifth trade—Short at 154¾, closing out on a quick dip to about 153, or at a point one-half of the preceding rally.

Sixth trade—Long at 154 (Rule 6).

Seventh trade—Long at 160¼ (Rule 3).

Eighth trade—Long at 156⅝ (technical adjustment on one-half preceding advance).

Ninth trade—Long at 160 (on technical adjustment—one-half preceding advance).

Tenth trade—Long at 165⅞.

Now we would better exercise caution and take profits on any sharp bulge.

Eleventh trade—Short at 171¼ (Rule 6) for good profits.

Twelfth trade—Short at 165½ (Rule 3) for about 7c., or to about 158½, or as far below 166 as it was above 166 (173½).

Thirteenth trade—Short at about 162-63, with a close Stop, say at 164, on theory that the rebound will extend to one-half of decline from 173⅛ (162⅞—12th).

Fourteenth trade—Short at 154 for about 146 (163-154½ equals 8½, or 146).

Sixteenth trade—Short at 146½ (Rule 3). Passing 147, expect 162⅞, minus 147, which equals 15⅞; 147, minus 15⅞, equals 131⅛ (reached 133¾).

Seventeenth trade—Short at 138. This will allow a chance to cover around 134-35.

You will observe that by playing the major swings only, according to Rules from May 17th to August 31st, a large aggregate of profits was indicated. A conservative estimate indicates a total of about 110c. Had we operated in only 5,000 bushels lots, the profits would have been 5,000 times $1.10, or $5,500; on 10,000 bushel lots, $11,000; and on 50,000 bushel lots, $55,000.

Now, assuming that a culmination price has been reached, we may look for a rebound equal to one-half of the decline from 173½ to 133¾, or to 153⅝ (reached 153⅞). I now leave the reader to work out the minor and major movements from 133¾ (August 1st) to the end of the option August 31st. This practice will prove helpful in understanding what has been explained up to this point. The reader, by going over the Wheat and Oats charts herein, will observe that the same laws of movements were in force there as in Corn. The charts herein of grain are accurate to the eighth of a cent. They were taken from the continuous quotations on the Chicago Board of Trade. A chart on Cotton would show the same laws are at work there as in grain, and that trades made in accordance therewith would work out the same as they are shown to have done in Corn. So, in the case of stocks, the same laws of movements are in operation and the Rules given herein apply to these in the same way as we have shown they apply in grain. Had there been any leading issue covering a considerable period of time in 1919 or 1920 on the stock board, a chart of the same would have been given in this work. Since there was not one, we shall have to content ourselves with a composite chart embracing about two dozen industrials. You will note that in the swings up and down, it shows that the laws of movements are always "on the job," as in grain, cotton, individual stocks, bonds, sugar, coffee and provisions.

After the reader has given due time and attention to familiarizing himself with the Rules set forth and explained herein, he will be well equipped to speculate successfully in stocks, grain and cotton.

Wheat Chart

In demonstrating the application of the Rules to the movements in Wheat, we shall apply them only to the major ones, leaving the student to seek information as to the application of the Rules to minor movements as carried out and explained in the Corn graphic shown on another page.

Our first application of a Rule to the Wheat movement occurs on the opening day, at 271½, when we sell short. We could buy at 262½ on the 16th and obtain a 2c. or 3c. profit, but we shall refrain from playing for small or moderate profits and operate only for larger or major profits.

We sell again at 259½ and close out (cover) our short commitments (271½, 159½) down near 254, 253, 252, 250 or possibly lower, but let us not be greedy. The decline has extended pretty far and in the natural order of movements a rebound is probable, equal to about one-half of the decline from 275 to 248 (275 minus 248 equals 27). One-half of the decline is 13½ and equals 261½. The adjustment price was approximately reached. We bought at 250½. Now we may take a chance of a short sale around 260-259 for a liberal profit. If we did not cover near 252-250, then we cover at 253½ and buy another lot, or buy twice the amount at 253½ that we sold short higher up. This transaction will give us a long trade with as large a lot as we sold short near 260-259. We will now try for a few cents advance, say to about 258.

Our next commitment will be a short sale at 247½. The movement from this point is likely to extend as far below 248, made on the 19th, as the distance from 248 to 275 (248 minus 27 equals 221). We will sell again at 232½ and hold for about 221. We now sell

NOTE—There was a closed wheat market from about 1917 to the 15th of July, 1920, when an open market was established or proclaimed by the Government Board that had authority to close the open market.

short again at 220½ and wait for a sharp, quick recession, then cover. We now buy at 210½ (August 2d) and try for a rebound equal to about one-half of the decline from 275 to 206½, or to about 240¾. We will take profits around 229-30. We buy again at 230½ and close out both trades at about 238-240 (reached 248). From 248 a setback to 232 is likely, this being one-half the distance from the preceding reaction 216 (August 4th), to 248 August 6th (reached 230). A purchase is now in order for a few cents advance (reached 246½). A reaction from this price should carry to about one-half the distance from 230 to 246½, or to 238¼ (reached 235½). Now a rally to a price one-half the distance from 246½ to 235½, or to 240¾ (reached 241¾).

Our next sale will be at 235. This trade should carry to about the distance below 235½ as the distance of 235½ to 246½, or to 224 (reached 226). We now buy at 230½ and accept a moderate profit. We could have followed this option until its expiration, but too much space would be required for a graphic showing all its fluctuations.

From what is shown in this chart, and the one of Corn, it would seem that any person possessing average perspicacity should be able to understand the laws of movements and how to apply the Rules in making a commitment in accordance therewith.

Some readers of this work may wonder why there is no graphic chart of a single Stock, or of Cotton, to be found herein. The reason for this is: There was no single representative stock that dominated the stock market movements in 1919-1920, so I have inserted a graphic chart showing the combined movements of about 25 Industrial stocks. This composite chart will serve to show the swings, and how true to form they have run over a period of two years. In the matter of Cotton, I did not have time to give it the attention required for accurate chart purposes. Besides, only a few of my patrons were interested in Cotton fluctuations.

The fluctuations shown in the Grain Charts are correct to the 16th of a cent, and serve to illustrate the law of movements in stocks and commodities. The movements in grain serve to illustrate these laws more clearly than do movements in stocks, because all movements in the stock market are more or less sympathetic, while in grain and cotton the movements are rarely sympathetic movements.

VIII
HOW TO GIVE ORDERS TO BROKERS

Opening an Account

After you have opened an account with your broker, you are ready to give him an order to buy or sell a stock or commodity. This may be done orally, in writing, by "phone" or by wire. It is well in cases where given over the 'phone to have the broker repeat the order back to you so as to insure against mistakes. Where a customer is in the broker's office when he gives his orders, he writes them on blank forms similar to the following:

John Doe & Co.,
6 John St.,

1. Buy for my account and risk ......shares of (name stock) at (name price)

or

2. Buy for my account and risk ....shares of .... at the market.

or

3. Sell for my a/c and risk .... shares of ....at .... (name price).

or

4. Sell for my a/c and risk.............shares of ....at the market.

If the order be for grain or provisions, then in place of shares, name the number of thousand bushels; or number of bbls., pounds, etc., and if for cotton, the number of bales you desire to buy or sell.

The above orders are good only for the day on which they are given, i. e., for the day named in the order. If you wish the order to remain "open" or continued over to the next day or until executed, then you may add to your order—"Open order," or K. G. C. which means—"keep good until cancelled." After your order has been executed, your broker should notify you, naming the price at which the stock or commodity is bought, or sold. Now you give him a Stop Loss order. (Every commitment should be protected by a Stop Loss order, since it limits possible losses). If it refers to the purchase under order No. 1 then make your Stop Loss order read:

5. "Sell on Stop for my account and risk....shares of (name stock) at ....(name price). We will suppose that order No. 1 was to buy 50 shares of Steel Com. at 102. If after it is bought you decide to place a Stop Loss at 99½, then your order will read: "Sell on Stop for my a/c and risk, 50 shares of Steel Com. at 99½." If it is desired to reverse the trade at the Stop Loss price, then instead of making the order read: "Sell 50 shares of Steel Com. at 99½ on Stop," you will make the order read:

6. "Sell for my a/c and risk 100 shares Steel Com. at 99½ on Stop." This order closes out the commitment of the 50 bought at 102 and puts you short of 50 for an anticipated further decline in price. Now, if you desire to recoup only the loss made on order No. 1, then you will give an order:

7. "Buy for my a/c and risk, 50 shares of Steel Com. at 96½." Such a price, if reached, will recoup the 2½ points loss on order No. 1, together with the broker's commission and transfer tax.

We will now suppose you wish to sell short, 50 shares of Steel at 102 and give your order accordingly. After execution of the order, you place a Stop Loss at say 103¾. So your order will read:

8. "Buy on Stop, 50 shares of Steel at 103¾," or if you desire to reverse the trade at that price then the order will read:

9. "Buy on Stop, 100 shares Steel Com. at 103¾." This order when executed puts you long of 50 shares.

We will now suppose that you are not near the ticker or in a broker's office, but desire to make a trade in accordance with Rule 3, you will then make your order read:

10. "Buy on Stop for my a/c and risk............ shares of .... at.............."

or

11. "Sell on Stop for my a/c and risk.......... shares of .... at.............."

In order No. 6, the selling price named will be below the present price, and in No. 8, above the price quoted when the order is given. (See Diagram explaining application of Rule 3.) Such orders may be for the day only, or as open orders (K. G. C.) Orders for the purchase or sale of grain, provisions and cotton may be made practically the same in form as in the case of stocks. (See orders numbered 1, 2, 3, 4, 5, 6, 7, 8, 9, 10 above.) Always make a memorandum of your orders for future execution, given your broker, and don't fail to renew the ones you desire to have executed, and to cancel those you decide you no longer desire to have executed.

Opening An Account

When you have decided to open an account with a stock broker, select a reliable one, usually a member of the N. Y. Stock Exchange.

If you select a broker who is not a member of the N. Y. Stock Exchange, not a member of the Chicago Board of Trade, nor a member of the Cotton Exchange, first ascertain as to his integrity and financial standing. Do not entrust him with one cent of your money until you are convinced after diligent inquiry and investigation that he is honest and trustworthy. If upon such investigation, you are satisfied the broker is all he should be, then you may deposit with him money or securities. You have thus opened an account with your broker and are prepared to give him orders to buy or sell stocks, bonds, grain, cotton, etc. on margin or for cash, but never on the partial payment plan. When your broker has bought or sold stocks, etc., on your order, he furnishes you with a memorandum of such purchase or sale, i. e., the name of the broker from whom you bought or to whom you sold. This serves as a confirmation of the purchase or sale. Bucket shops and brokers who bucket their customers' trades, do not furnish their customers with such a memorandum. When you close out the transaction, by selling in the case of a former purchase, or buying to cover a short trade, you receive another memorandum giving the name of the broker to whom sold or from whom bought.

Your broker will, from time to time, usually on the first of each month, furnish you with a statement showing profits and losses on commitments made by you during the preceding month. You may at any time ask for a statement of your account, and you may close out your account at any time. Always keep a memorandum of all the trades you make so that you can compare them with the brokers' statement of your account.

If you deposit $500, then you should limit your trades to 10 or 20 shares. If $1,000, then 20 to 40 shares; $3,000—50 shares and not over 100 shares; $4,000, 100 shares. If you have deposited all of your available capital, then instead of 20 shares on $500 capital, make your initial trades 10 shares. This will allow you to make a second trade on a reverse movement or in another stock, and allow something for possible losses. Besides, you are not so likely to get "tied up" when operating conservatively. The average uninitiated trader would be disposed to trade in 50 shares on a $500 account and thus have only a 10 point margin to protect the trade. If a loss of 2 or 3 points follows, then he would be obliged to trade in smaller lots thereafter.

IX
MARKET PSYCHOLOGY

Mystery
The Known and Unknown
The Unknown in Its Relation to the Markets
The Crowd Mind
Mental Suggestion

Speculation being a mental effort or operation, it is important that we understand how the human mind acts in its relation to market movements and affairs marketwise. The composite mind acts pretty much as the individual mind. There are individuals whose mental attitude is typical of the mental mood of the crowd mind; so, the actions, expressions, opinions of such a "type" are usually wrong marketwise. If such a person makes a commitment in the market, it serves as a valuable "tip" for the skilled speculator to "copper" the "type's" trade, i .e., sell when the "type" buys; buy when he sells. If he expresses the opinion that the market or a particular stock, or commodity is a purchase, profitable results are likely to follow on a short scale. If he is bearish, then a purchase is in order. The theory on which this assumption is predicated is this: The "type" is a "susceptible" subject for mental suggestion. He is easily swayed or convinced (unconsciously) by what he reads or hears, so he naturally gives out what he has unconsciously absorbed. What he sucked in was inspired by those whose financial interests were likely to be benefited if acted on by the type or the composite mind that absorbed the suggestion. This is why the crowd or outside public is nearly always wrong marketwise.

Mystery

The human mind entertains much interest in mystery. It excites hope and fear. The insiders or manipulators play on the moods of the outsiders by hints of some secret action relating to a stock, as that a "melon" is to be cut; that valuable rights are to be offered; that an increase in dividends is probable; that a stock dividend may be declared, etc., etc. The public is always a willing dupe where mystery plays a part in the speculative game. It willingly pays the price for being hum-bugged.

The Known and Unknown

The human mind is more interested in the unknown than in the known. So it is said, anticipation gives more pleasure, or pain than realization. When the unknown becomes the known, anticipated pleasure decreases and fear diminishes or vanishes. This is also true marketwise. This is why we are always striving to unveil the unknown. When the unknown becomes the known in the market, a reverse movement usually follows. It is often said: "The market is discounting some good news or some bad news." When the so-called "good news" is made public, the Insiders sell to the outsiders; when the "bad news" comes out, then the insiders buy from the public what it sells on the publication of the "bad news." The mystery which interests and attracts the average stock and commodity gambler is of the superficial kind; the sort that requires little thinking, and no reasoning. It is of the kind related to the throwing of dice or the bet on the turn of a coin or card. In short, it is akin to that which appeals to the child mind.

The Unknown in Its Relation to the Markets

Fear is man's worst enemy. It is the bete noir that stands before him and bars his way on the road to SUCCESS. It has been the cause of nearly all of man's failures. It is the duty of every man to eradicate this unreasonable emotion from his mind and substitute COURAGE.

The UNKNOWN—when it appears to the mind as possessing the power for harm—causes FEAR or a temporary dethronement of reasoning powers. When this UNKNOWN becomes the KNOWN, then fear disappears and reason reasserts itself. A superstitious person who believes in ghosts is quite likely to see such apparitions in lonely spots, as for instance, in or near a grave yard on dark nights. If he has courage sufficient to approach the imaginary spirits and touch them he will likely find them some living domestic animals or rocks or stumps or posts, usually light in color. The moment he touches these tangible objects, his fear vanishes as quickly as do the ghosts he saw a moment before. So, in market operations, man fears anything not definitely known that threatens to harm or injure prices. He permits fear to dethrone reason temporarily and his impulse is to sell his stocks regardless of prices, and usually at the lowest prices. Of course this particular man is not an exceptional one. He represents the crowd, so we find all men are inclined to act as he has done and this precipitates a severe break in the market. Now when this UNKNOWN that caused a panic in his brain (and in the brains of other fellow men) becomes the KNOWN then prices of stocks rise and usually quite as rapidly and violently as they fell. The lowest prices on a "scare" occurs at that moment immediately preceding the UNKNOWN becoming the KNOWN. The scare then vanishes. The ghosts have been transformed into some light colored animate or inanimate bodies. That particular moment is the psychological one at which to BUY STOCKS for BIG PROFITS. This is where the man with courage jumps in and seizes OPPORTUNITY by the forelock.

Now on the other hand, whatever is anticipated of a pleasing or desirable character is seldom realized in full measure. Applying this mental state to market operations: Whenever some particular thing—calculated to improve the prices of a stock, the exact nature of which is more or less of a mystery—is being anticipated by a rise in the price of the stock, and this mysterious something becomes definitely known, then a reverse movement may be expected and sales are in order for profits proportionate to the rise based on the UNKNOWN.

Mystery has a fascination for the human mind. The movements or fluctuations in stocks, grain and cotton markets are a mystery to the average men, thus the curiosity of the public to take a chance in the game. To the person who understands the laws of market movements, there is little mystery in speculation. He knows about the KNOWN and the UNKNOWN and their intimate relationship. Fear finds no place in his brain to plant its baneful germs. COURAGE, born of a knowledge of natural laws and their workings in market movements, brings him success where the crowd fails. So, every triumph of the WILL as against FEAR tends to double a permanent habit of COURAGE and to bring SUCCESS.

The Crowd Mind

This is a composite mental state or attitude regarding any belief, theory or subject. I shall deal briefly with this mental state in its relation to the stock and commodity markets:

When we find the so-called crowd—*i. e.*, the public—bullish or bearish on the market, this signifies that the composite mind entertains an almost unanimous sentiment that the market will go higher or that prices will decline further.

You have doubtless met that person who tells you: "When I buy them, they go down. When I sell them, they go up." Now, that unfortunate person has the crowd mind. He thinks and acts with the crowd. That's why he buys when he should sell, and vice versa. The crowd is always 75% wrong marketwise. Were it otherwise, the market would be unprofitable to the Insiders. It is essential that the public (the crowd) be wrong in order that the Insiders may make profits. But why should the public be nearly always wrong? Why not right at least one-half of the time?

Here is the explanation in a nutshell—the crowd mind is an unthinking mind, so is easily influenced. It reads the venal press, principally newspapers. What it reads agrees with the selfish interests of the readers, therefore it is acceptable. An opinion is thus formed and action in accordance therewith follows. The readers of this inspired news or information do not realize that it is mental suggestion, pure and simple, and is carried in this or other agencies for the very purpose of putting the public wrong on the market. If you tell a man something that agrees with his opinion or belief, or that promises to profit his personal interests, or that tickles his vanity, he will readily and gladly accept what you thus proffer even though it be untrue and against his interests. While on the other hand, if you tell him something that does not agree with his inclination or belief, or that would be likely to cause him pain, loss or injury, he would harken with ill-concealed displeasure and then discard it, although all that was told him was true and carried with it the best of advice.

The crowd mind is disposed to be as one—at extremes. That is to say, at the top of a substantial forward movement and at or near the bottom of a downward movement. At those points, the crowd soon becomes dissipated or scattered and does not reform until another extreme is reached.

An illustration of what can be done with the crowd mind was evidenced in the fictitious and artificial bull market of 1919-20. The big interests canvassed the situation from a money-making standpoint early in

1919, when stocks were at the bottom of a big preceding decline. They reasoned something like this: The public, the silk shirt munition workers, the profiteers, the shop keepers and grain and cotton growers have made a surplus of money which they are itching to spend recklessly, so we will set in motion inspiring bullish "news" in "literature," newspaper and financial periodicals. They carried out the planned campaign through adroit manipulation of the most flagrant character. The public was enticed into the trap and "fleeced." Few of the innocent and unsuspecting victims escaped.

The Insiders, through inspired news, rumors, and other agencies create the crowd sentiment and then profit by it. When the crowd is acting enthusiastically on an advance or on a decline, that is the time to make a commitment for a reverse movement.

Mental Suggestion

The mind of the average person moves along on the lines of least resistance. Mental effort is laborious and distasteful. This is one reason why the movies are popular. It is this mental laziness that leads the public into error marketwise. The public prefers to obtain its information on the market by the easiest possible method, so it acts on mental suggestion furnished through brokers' letters, advertisements, newspapers, financial periodicals, circulars and rumors relating to matters marketwise. The mind of the inexperienced in market affairs may be compared to that of the nine-year-old child in worldly affairs.

Something for nothing; much for little. These are the magic words that make a strong appeal to the unsuspecting and inexperienced mind. They find a ready and welcome reception in the minds of avaricious or covetous persons. Such persons prove easy victims for the swindler who promises much beyond a reasonable return on an investment. Boston recently furnished an example of how an ex-convict "confidenced" the public to the tune of several millions on a get-rich-quick scheme for a promise of 50% profit in 45 days. He employed mystery, and appealed to GREED. Guard against mental suggestion as you would against poison or a deadly enemy.

X
INSIDE INFORMATION

Inside Interests
Market Advice
Economics
Statistics
Greed
Market News
Percentage
Paragraphs

"There ain't no such animal." It ranks with the sea serpent and ghosts. There are persons who claim to have seen a sea serpent and others who declare they have seen ghosts. There are doubtless many persons who believe there are such animals as sea serpents and thousands who are firm in their belief that there are such things as animated spirits.

The general public believes that so-called "inside information" leaks and is obtainable by a select few of favored persons to be disseminated among their friends or patrons. So-called inside information is given out at times but it's of a kind with a motive (usually sinister) behind it. Sometimes it "makes good" (for a purpose) and at other times it fails to work out profitably for the recipients. In any case, it's safer to refrain from accepting such unauthentic information (?).

Does it seem reasonable that the pools or insiders who are manipulating stocks or commodities with the object of making money at the expense of the public or outsiders, would make known to an outsider what they are doing or intend doing? Does the General of an army make known his plans and purposes to the General of an enemy army? Of course not! Yet there are those who are so credulous as to believe that inside information is obtainable and will be furnished to outsiders for a consideration. The only inside information I have ever been able to obtain came through that little instrument called the TICKER. It is the only reliable and authentic source of inside information. This little instrument records on the tape what the Insiders are doing.

Inside Interests or Insiders

These comprise a group of mysterious persons unknown to the outside public, who, through their personal financial resources and their close and intimate association with the banking interest, are enabled to make markets to suit their personal interests. These are personages who "mark the cards" before they are "laid on the table."

These are the men who prepare inspired "news" to be circulated through various channels and agencies for the purpose of misleading the public marketwise. They control the markets. What they are actually doing is revealed through the ticker, and in no other way.

Market Advice

Advice or suggestions are most acceptable when they agree with one's interest, inclinations or opinions. Advice that is contrary to one's wishes, hopes and personal interests is unacceptable even though it be of the best. Policy says: "Give 'em what they want." Honesty says: "Give 'em what they need."

Advice on stocks and commodities and on market movements may be classified into GOOD, BAD and WORST.

GOOD ADVICE is so rare that not more than one out of a million persons is capable of giving it. Persons capable of giving good and reliable advice marketwise are those who are self reliant, independent and original in thought and action. The services of such men command an income of from $15,000 to $30,000 yearly. Such persons do not serve for wages or a salary.

BAD ADVICE is POPULAR advice. It is usually furnished FREE of charge. It is of the kind that the public craves and accepts. Whatever advices coincide with public opinion is invariably wrong, so is logically bad. It does not require ability to give out bad advice, and that is perhaps why so many are giving it out—usually FREE.

WORST ADVICE is inspired, *i. e.*, given out by the Insiders through newspapers, financial periodicals and other agencies for the purpose of misleading the public. BROKERS' ADVICE—Little reliance should be placed on the opinion of brokers. Their advice marketwise is usually biased by self interest. Their opinions generally coincide with those of the public, and since the public is 75% to 95% wrong, the advice of brokers averages about 5% right.

Not one broker or banker in a hundred is qualified to advise knowingly on *stocks*, *grain* or *cotton*. Brokers and bankers may have opinions and these may at times be worthy of consideration, but the value of their advice on speculative movements of stocks and commodities is negligible, for the reason that very few brokers or bankers are acquainted with the *science of speculation*, i. e., with the laws of market movements.

Brokers are prone to advise purchases rather than short sales. First, because they know the public prefers to buy rather than to sell short. Second, knowing that their profits come principally from such customers, brokers usually have a " one way " opinion on stocks and commodities. Don't blame 'em—it's human nature. They are in the game to make money just as is the customer.

BANKERS' ADVICE:—May be considered of a negative quality. About the only advice of value that comes through banks is via the "higher up" officials of the Metropolitan Banks who co-operate with pools and use the banks' funds to help the pools "put over" something for mutual profits. If the pools succeed—all's well with the officials. If they fail—the loss is likely to be entered in the bank's profit and loss account.

PRESS ADVICE—When newspapers and financial publications "*suggest*" for purchase certain stocks which are specifically referred to, *caveat emptor* applies. In other words, whoever buys such "*suggested*" stocks will later on regret having "*paid the freight*" (penalty) for his credulity. Small calibre financial periodicals get the largest part of their revenue from these questionable methods. Two or three daily newspapers in N. Y. "work" their readers through "SUGGESTION" methods.

The pools arrange with the little fellows connected with the newspapers to write special items extolling the merits of certain stocks which these pools are manipulating for the purpose of unloading on the "outside public." The pools "divvy" profits with the financial paragraphers. Better steer clear of these false beacons and close your ears to the voices of the Sirens.

FREE ADVICE is generally the most expensive in the end. Beware of those poisonous "Stinging bugs"—called "tips."

Economics

A knowledge of the phenomena arising out of man's activities in the acquisition and use of wealth should be understood by all who operate in the stock and commodity markets. Where there is an effect, there is a cause, and vice versa. Knowledge perceives cause and anticipates effect. The phenomena alluded to above are natural laws. These are always active, although at times seemingly passive or inactive. They are in constant operation to establish an equilibrium. When these laws are not violated, market prices are natural or regular. When violated, prices become artificial, irregular, excited, erratic, abnormal. These violations may be produced by manipulation, legislation, fear, greed. Natural laws are immutable and work out in an orderly way if not violated, but when violated, exact a penalty commensurate with the disturbance or interruption. Thus it happens that when violent fluctuations occur in the markets in an upward swing or in a downward swing, reverse extreme or excited movements follow. In short, extremes are followed by others proportionate in the opposite direction. This law of extremes may be observed in nature. For example: An extended period of hot, dry weather is usually followed by a violent rain storm. So an abnormal period of wet weather is generally succeeded by a "dry spell" of equal extent. A balance or an average is thus established. Good times are followed by bad times and vice versa to establish an average. Extremely high prices of farm products are followed by abnormally low prices and vice versa. Moral: Make hay while the sun shines, i. e., buy when prices are low; sell when prices are high. Provide against the inevitable rainy day.

Statistics

This term as applied to stocks means those facts that can be stated in numbers, or in tables of numbers, or in any tabular and classified arrangement. Statistics is overworked and more stress put upon it than its importance justifies as a stock market factor. What a stock has earned in the past as a basis for determining its probable earnings in the future would perhaps be of value in normal times when conditions do not vary materially over a series of months or even years, but when conditions are changing from month to month and the future can not be reckoned with approximate probability, statistics is of little value in determining whether a stock is a purchase or a sale. So, the chances are he who bases his commitments on such information is likely to go astray marketwise. Statistics and "book value" have caused many believers therein to suffer severe losses.

The prices of active stocks do not always adjust themselves to statistics. They move about as the pools or cliques decide they shall move regardless of statistics. They may be manipulated far above their intrinsic value or depressed far below their statistical value.

It is well to keep constantly in mind the fact that stocks are speculative and are bounced up and down for profits. The fact that speculation is a scientific game should not be disregarded. If there are persons who have not yet realized the foregoing facts, the sooner they become disillusioned, the better for themselves. The average trader or investor in stocks is likely to be influenced to some degree by the dividend rate of the stock as a measure of its price or value. Commitments predicated on such a theory are misleading, since stocks do not always harmonize with their dividend rates. If you would verify or confirm this assertion, run through the stock list on the N. Y. Stock Exchange. What such an inspection reveals may cause surprise. You will find some of the stocks quoted therein showing bargain prices according to statistics. You will find some stocks paying no dividend, selling near 100 and others in the same class selling as low as 5; while others pay 4% to 10% dividend rates selling at a 12% or 20% dividend yield. There are always reasons for such seeming "out of line" prices. In the first instances cited above (near 100) a 6% or 8% dividend is perhaps expected to be declared in the near future. In the second case, there is a doubt as to the present rate being continued. In short, it is anticipated that the present rate may be reduced or passed. There are times when,—as in a big bull market, nearly all active stocks sell temporarily at prices disproportionately above fair dividend rates, or dividend yield. So there are times in a bear market, when nearly all stocks sell at prices lower than their dividend rates seem to justify. The far-sighted man sells his stocks when the market price shows a low dividend investment return and buys when the price gives a return on the investment above the regular dividend rate. When speculating in active stocks, one would do well to avoid statistics.

The more one reads them, the farther one is from the real or present market. Whenever I see a man consulting statistics relating to the market, I know that man does not understand the speculative game; that he is at least 30 years behind the present date. He is like the man who reads the news slips handed around in brokers' offices every few minutes from 10.30 A. M. to 3 P. M. for guidance marketwise, and does not realize that the profits made off such "news" are shown on the ticker tape already in the ticker basket. Statistics and "news" are to the market what thunder is to lightning. Genuine news is like lightning from a clear sky—something unexpected. Statistics may be likened unto the water that has passed over the dam. If the land tributary to the stream is being denuded of its trees, then the dam will not be regular in its flow or supply of water, i. e., too much in the spring; too little in the summer and fall. Conditions are constantly changing in every way and these cannot always be accurately measured, gauged or forecasted.

I recall the time when Am. Sugar was a very active stock and a favorite with speculators. I recollect when St. Paul Common was *the* active favorite, selling near 200. So U. P. above 200; N. H. was once a favorite, around 250. So Steel Com. was 38 in 1915 with no dividend, and 136⅝ in 1917, with a 17% dividend disbursement. The former standing of these and some others was impaired in 1920. They have surrendered their primacy and have been supplanted by newer favorites. Time brings with it extraordinary and unexpected changes.

The past and the present make the future, so we must be prepared to meet the future as it is being shaped by the past and the present, and we must act in harmony with the changes as they are developing. So far as the market is concerned, the ticker tape must be our guide if we are to profit by unexpected changes. As a matter of fact nearly all changes in the market are unlooked for ones, i. e., unexpected and unanticipated. The movements in stocks are more or less surprises or disappointments. They advance when a decline is expected and decline when an advance is forecasted. The unexpected is either strategic or tactical. Movements are made to deceive the followers and thus capture from them what they expected and hoped to obtain from their captors—PROFITS. The tactics and strategy employed in speculation are similar to those in military manoeuvers—to deceive, surprise, capture. When pools set out to advance or depress a stock, they do not consult statistics to guide them. They usually act contrary to what statistics indicates. In this way they surprise and overthrow the statistician and his followers.

Greed

An avaricious or keen desire for profits is one of the most prevalent causes of failure in speculation. This weakness is general among traders. They desire "just a little more" profit. If the stock or commodity bought advances, then that's proof to them that it will advance further and so they hang on. They

NOTE:—Statistics based on reports furnished by Standard Oil Corporations are perhaps the most reliable of all statistics relating to production of oil.

usually overstay and thus miss their market. If they fail to obtain the top price and it reacts, then they assure or console themselves by the expression: "Oh, it will come back." It may "come back" but often it does not, and instead, declines to below the purchase price and frequently results in a loss. The same observations apply to a short sale for a further anticipated decline. It is good policy to be satisfied with a reasonable profit and be willing to leave some for the other fellow. The market is always there and other opportunities for making profits will present themselves while the greedy trader is waiting to get the last eighth.

Greed leads to disaster in another way. A speculator has started in to buy at the inception of a bull movement. He makes money. The more he makes, the more avaricious he becomes as the market moves forward. His confidence in himself increases until he develops a mental state known in the vernacular as "big head" or "swelled head." He now has unbounded confidence in himself and "plays the limit." Soon thereafter the market culminates at the top and the trend reverses, but Mr. Swelled Head is ignorant of this, so continues to buy on set-backs instead of selling on rallies. A drastic slump follows and Mr. B. H. goes to the scrap pile—BUSTED.

Market News

Market news relates to something that was before unknown. It applies or refers to something likely to affect the market. The average so-called news is not such news as will benefit the public marketwise, because it is already known and has been used or acted upon by the Insiders. After action by the Insiders the "news" is passed to the outsiders who act on it as did the Insiders, but usually with a reverse or adverse result. If the "news" be "good," then the market usually sells off, and if "bad," it advances. So, the proverbial saying: "On good news the market declines; on bad news, it advances." This seems paradoxical, but it is perfectly logical. The Insiders who use the good news to advance a stock or commodity are ready to sell when the good news is given out to the public. There is then more selling than buying, i. e., there is a preponderance of selling, and the result is a decline. A like result occurs on bad news, i. e., an advance instead of a decline. News calculated to affect the market should be accepted cum grano salis. Usually "news" that is given out in printed form during market hours is of little value to the outsider, and if acted on in harmony with its tenor, is likely to cause him who operates on it to regret his ill-advised action. The most accurate and reliable market "news" comes through the ticker. By the time it is out in printed form for public consumption, a record of the profits made on the ticker news is in the ticker basket. Important news (notably political) is generally kept sequestered in "storage" for a time, in order to allow the Insiders to skim the cream off before the public is permitted to partake of the milk.

Bucket Shop

A bucket shop is ostensibly a broker's office with a manager assuming to be a legitimate broker. Such a concern neither buys nor sells for its customers. It merely bets with its victims. If the customer bets a stock or a commodity is going up, the bucket shop accepts the bet, i. e., bets the customer it is going down. Many self-styled brokers do a bucket business. Nearly all of the extravagant advertising concerns that specialize in low-priced, unlisted or Curb stocks, or operate on the partial payment plan, or sell Puts and Calls may be considered as bucket shops. The customer (victim) who patronizes such "brokers" is likely to lose every dollar he deposits with these parasites.

A Few Examples in Percentage

A stock at par (100) pays a dividend of 4% and is selling at 58. What is the dividend yield at that price? Divide 4,000 by 58 equals 7.9%.

At what price shall I buy a 4% stock to return 6% on the investment? Divide 4,000 by 6 equals 66⅝.

A 6% stock is selling at 108. What is the dividend yield? Divide 6 by 108 equals 5½%.

Which brings the larger return on the investment, a 5% bond bought at 80, or a 7% bond bought at 111¾? Divide 5,000 by 80 equals 6¼. Divide 7,000 by 111.75 equals 6¼ plus. About the same.

How large a sum shall I be obliged to invest in a 6% bond to bring me an income of $3,000 a year? Divide $3,000 by $.06 equals $50,000.

A buys 100 shares of Steel Common at 90 on margin. He deposits with his broker $2,000. He holds the stock 20 days then sells it. What is the amount of the interest charge on the transaction with a call money rate of 8%? One hundred shares at 90 equals $9,000. A furnished $2,000 and his broker $7,000 to finance the transaction. The interest on $7,000 at 8% for a year is $560. For a month, 1/12 of 560 or $46.66, and for 1 day, 1/30th of 46.66 or $1.56 and for 20 days, $1.56 times 20 or $31.20.

Practical Paragraphs

Beware of "inside" tips to buy or sell a named stock.

Beware of "good things" proffered by quondam friends.

You would better not accept market advice from friends inexperienced in market affairs.

When you find yourself building castles on indicated or prospective profits, accept the profits in sight—at once.

If your opinion disagrees with the tape, discard or reverse your opinion.

When the market looks as though going much higher, convert your paper profits into cash. When it appears to be going much lower, cover shorts.

When your exhilaration over paper profits is above par, convert such paper profits into cash immediately.

If it is easy to do, don't. If it seems like throwing your money away, do it.

The market seldom does what it is expected to do. If it did what the public expected, the Insiders would fare poorly.

Every movement in the market is made with the purpose of beating the outsider.

The human mind is so constituted that advancing prices cause exhilaration, while declining prices cause mental depression. Thus it is, advancing prices lure the public into buying what the Insiders or promoters have to sell.

Large lots at advancing prices do not necessarily prove that the stock or commodity showing them will advance materially higher, nor that large lots in a declining market mean still lower prices.

An abnormal volume of transactions after a substantial movement in the upward or in the downward direction means a reverse trend is near at hand.

Every game requiring mental skill can be mastered and beaten.

Stocks and commodities are manipulated upward to unload on the outside public.

Stocks are made to sell.

Never deposit money with or send money to a broker or exploiter until you have made an investigation as to his integrity, reliability and financial rating.

Never buy stocks of unknown value from a salesman who calls and importunes you to buy, unless he can furnish you with unquestionable credentials and evidence that he is authorized to act as agent for a reputable principal.

Buy no stock or bond for investment without first making an investigation as to its value and safety.

Avoid being greedy; accept reasonable profits.

The bull makes profits; so also the bear, but the hog generally loses all he had in sight.

Guard against overconfidence. When you are dead sure"—STOP! LOOK! LISTEN!

When stocks or commodities are moving in a given direction they usually end the movement by a quick spurt in the upward direction, and a quick sharp dip in the downward direction.

Always operate in the features or leaders both in the upward and in the downward direction. Other members of the same group to which the leader or feature belongs will act in sympathy with the leader, but follow the leader, i. e., buy or sell the leader rather than the sympathizers.

For example: If Steel Common is the active feature or leader upward, buy it rather than other members of the Steel group—Republic, Beth. B., Lack., etc. So if Mexican Pete is the leading active issue in the upward direction, buy it rather than Pan. Am., Royal D., Cal. Pete. or other oil stocks, and if Mex. Pete. is the active leader in the downward direction, sell it instead of the other oil issues that naturally act sympathetically

---

Don't buy or sell an inactive stock, nor one that moves over a narrow range.

Do not try to anticipate the movement of an inactive stock. If you do, the chances are it will disappoint you.

Every game has definite rules for playing it. These are based on the laws of chance.

Never try to guess the market—that's gambling. Be sure you are playing it according to a definite rule, then make the commitment.

Keep with the trend of the market.

What grows rapidly is generally short lived. This rule applies also to market movements.

Reaction is equal to action.

Apply salt to "sure things" and "news."

The harder it is for you to make a trade, the surer the probable profit. If it seems easy, let it pass.

Never plunge unless you understand the game well.

Never buy a stock because it seems "cheap," nor sell it short just because it seems "too high." Things are not always what they seem.

If you would have your brain serve you profitably, you should feed it with proper mental food.

The market seems strongest at its weakest points (tops) and weakest at its strongest points (bottom).

A man may be excused for making some mistakes, but to make the same mistake repeatedly puts him in the fool class.

Don't confine your operations to a single issue unless it is a leading feature.

Slow movements are safer to follow than fast ones. Such movements usually end with a spurt in the upward direction and a quick dip in the downward direction.

When a stock or commodity opens on a range at a price above and below the preceding day's top or bottom close, anticipate a reverse movement.

Beware of so-called "book value." It is of little or no value marketwise.

One extreme is followed by another in the opposite direction—and usually with the same intensity.

MARKET GLOSSARY

ABBREVIATIONS—These are the symbols used to designate the stocks and commodities quoted on the tape. For example: A, for Atchison; BO, Baltimore & Ohio; Ca, Canadian Pacific; CO, Chesapeake and Ohio; St. Paul; E, Erie; GQ, Great Northern pfd; CEN, N. Y. Central; N. P., Northern Pacific; PA, Pennsylvania R. R.; U, Union Pacific; ABS, Am. Beet Sugar; BL, Baldwin Locomotive; MN, Mexican Petroleum; X, U. S. Steel Corp., etc., etc.

AT THE MARKET—Is an order to the broker to buy or sell at the current price.

AT THE OPENING—Is an order to the broker to buy or sell at the best price obtainable after the opening of the market.

AVERAGING—Buying or selling against the trend of the market.

BEAR—One who believes or anticipates a decline in prices of stocks or commodities is occurring or is about to occur.

BEAR MARKET—One in which the selling preponderates and prices decline.

BID AND ASKED PRICE—The price offered and the price asked for a stock or commodity.

BLANKET MORTGAGE—One that covers a group or class of different pieces of property in one general lien.

BLIND POOL—Is a combine of a limited number of persons to act for many who deposit their funds or securities with discretionary power given the members of the pool to act without reporting to their principals until the object for which the pool was created has been consummated.

BOOKS CLOSE—A date named before the dividend is paid. Transferring of stock from that date stops until a date named after dividend is paid.

BOOKS OPEN—This is the date on which the books are opened after the dividend has been paid or a transfer made.

BORROWING STOCKS—This is generally done by lending their equivalent in money. If the stocks are scarce, they usualy command a premium of 1/16 and upward, depending upon the demand for them.

BREAK—A drastic or sudden recession in prices.

BULGE—An advance in price beyond the preceding high point.

BULL—One who believes stocks or commodities are advancing or are about to advance.

BULL MARKET—An advancing market with a preponderance of buying orders.

BUYING ON A SCALE—Purchases made at named prices on advancing quotations.

BUYING OUTRIGHT—Purchasing a stock or commodity for cash and paying the full market price.

BUY ON STOP—This is an order given the broker to buy at a price named above the prevailing or current price. Such an order is usually given to stop losses on a short sale.

CALL—A contract entitling the holder to demand delivery of a stock or commodity at a designated price above the current price before such contract expires.

CALL LOAN—A loan payable on demand.

CALL MONEY—Money lent with the understanding that it is to be repaid on demand.

CARRYING CHARGES—These are what the broker exacts from his clients for interest and other charges advanced by the broker to complete payment for securities bought for his client.

CLIQUE—Is in some respects the same as a pool. It is a combination of a limited number of persons to advance or depress stocks or commodities.

CLOSING PRICE—The price at which the last sale was made prior to the closing of the market.

COLLATERAL—In market operations, this term designates securities deposited in lieu of cash.

COMMON STOCK—A stock which is entitled to dividends only after the Preferred stock, bonds and other prior obligations have been paid.

CORNER—The state of things produced by a combination of persons who buy up or control the whole or available part of any stock or commodity which compels those who need such stock or commodity, to buy it at an artificial price.

COUPON—A certificate of interest due, printed at the bottom of transferrable bonds, given for a term of years, designed to be cut off and presented for payment when the interest is due—(Web. Int. Dic.)

COVER—When short sellers of stocks or commodities buy to complete the transaction they are said to "cover shorts."

CREDIT BALANCE—The balance remaining to the customer's credit after all legitimate charges have been deducted.

CURB MARKET—A market on the Street. The N. Y. Curb market on Board Street is the principal one in the U. S.

DEBIT BALANCE—A balance that is due the broker by the client after his account is balanced.

DELIVERY—The actual transfer from one broker or a customer to another.

DIP—A moderate set-back or decline in the price of a stock or commodity.

DISCRETIONARY ORDER—An order given a broker or one acting as agent for another to buy or sell at his discretion.

DISCRETIONARY POOL—A combination of individuals given authority to act for others on their own motion to buy and sell stocks or commodities.

DIVIDEND—The share of a sum divided that falls to each individual as a share holder.

DRIVE—A concerted action by several, combined to depress the price of a stock or several stocks or commodities.

EX-DIVIDEND—A stock or bond is said to sell ex-dividend when the amount of the current dividend is taken off the price of the stock.

EX-RIGHTS—When the right to buy a stock has been exercised the price of the rights is taken off the price of the stock; the stock is then said to be selling ex-rights.

FEATURE—Is a stock more active than others in the general list.

FLAT—A trade without interest or commission.

FLYER—Taking a chance in the market on some particular stock through a purchase or a sale for quick profits.

FOREIGN EXCHANGE—The process of settling accounts or debts between parties of different countries without the intervention of money.

FRACTIONAL LOTS—One or more shares of stock of less than 100 shares. (See under ODD LOTS.)

FUTURES—Values of commodities named, to be delivered in subsequent months as in cereals, cotton, sugar, coffee, pork, lard, ribs, etc.

G. T. C. ORDER—Means "good until cancelled."

GUNNING—When two or more brokers combine their efforts to dislodge a long or a short trade held by another, either by depressing or advancing the price of the same, they are said to be gunning for such stock.

INACTIVE STOCKS—These are stocks in which there is no active public demand and therefore are more or less dormant.

INDUSTRIALS—Stocks based on manufacturing plants of various kinds.

IRREGULAR—The market is said to be irreguar when some stocks move in one direction while others move in the opposite direction.

LAMB—Is an unsuspecting, inexperienced and unsophisticated buyer of stocks or commodities. Persons who buy irrospective of value or price.

LIQUIDATING—Selling long stock in considerable volume.

LONG STOCK—A stock held in anticipation of an advance in price.

LONG PULL—Buying or selling a stock or commodity with the intention of holding it some time in anticipation of obtaining a substantial profit on the transaction.

MANIPULATION—Artificial operations in the market to cause advancing or declining quotations.

MARGIN—This term is applied to a part of the purchase price, or in the case of selling short, a part of the selling price. This plan of trading enables the operator to buy or sell a larger quantity of stocks or commodities than by buying outright. It is the popular and general method of trading on Exchanges.

MARKET PRICE—The price at which a stock or commodity is selling when the order is given to buy or sell.

NON-CUMULATIVE—Not cumulative. A preferred stock is said to be non-cumulative when not under an obligation to pay lapsed or unpaid dividends before the common stock can share in dividends.

NO PAR VALUE—Means without named par value instead of a fixed face value.

ODD LOTS—Lots of less than regular lots. The unit of trading in stocks on the N. Y. Stock Exchange is 100 shares. In cereals, 5,000 bushels is the unit on the Chicago Board of Trade.

OPEN ORDER—An order to buy or sell a stock or commodity when the price reached is that named in the order. It is in effect until cancelled.

OPTION—See FUTURES.

PAPER PROFITS—The profits indicated on the quotation board or on the tape.

PAR VALUE—Is the amount named on the face of the certificate issued. The par value does not establish the price of the stock. It may sell much above or much below.

PLUNGE—Buying or selling a quantity of stocks or commodities on margin disproportionate to one's capital. Taking big chances; a gamble.

POINT—A movement of $1.00 a share in stocks.

POINTER—A suggestion to buy or sell.

POOL—A combination of two or more persons banded together for the purpose of advancing or depressing a stock or commodity for their personal profit and the profit of those interested with them in such operations.

PREFERRED STOCK—One taking precedence of minor ones of the same company.

PROMOTER—One who devotes his activities personally or by advertisements to advance the sale of stock. A sort of schemer.

PUT—Is an agency by which, for a consideration, one person acquires the right to deliver or "put" a stock or commodity to another at a fixed price within a specified time.

PYRAMIDING—Buying or selling with the principal and accumulated profits combined—usually with a small profit on each transaction. It is practically building a pyramid with the apex downward, and so is easily toppled over. Only gamblers operate on such a hazardous plan.

QUOTATION—The current price of a stock, bond or commodity.

Rally—A moderate rebound after a decline of a stock or commodity.

Reaction—A movement in the opposite direction of the trend, usually applied to a movement opposite to that of a rally.

Realizing or Taking Long Profits—Means that a bull is selling stocks or commodities to take profits.

Recovery—A coming back after a temporary recession in the prices of stocks or commodities.

Rights—A privilege given to stock holders to subscribe to a new issue of the same stock.

Scalp—Buying and selling for fractional profits.

Sell on Stop—An order given the broker to sell at a named price below the current price.

Short—Is a trade made in anticipation of a lower price.

Short Selling—Selling a stock or commodity not owned by the seller but in expectation that it can be bought for delivery at a lower price and with a profit on such short sale.

Spread—Is a privilege to buy or sell a stock or commodity at a named price above and below the current price. It is a Put and a Call combined.

Squeezing Shorts—A combination of operators cooperating together for the purpose of advancing stocks and commodities in order to force short sellers to buy back at a higher price than that at which they sold short.

Stock Dividends—A transfer to stock holders of an additional issue of stock or of part of the original shares.

Stop Loss—An order to the broker to limit a possible loss on a transaction by purchase or sale. It is a sort of insurance against larger losses.

Street Certificate—Certificate of stock endorsed by the owner and guaranteed by a responsible broker, that passes without transfer on the company's books.

Technical Adjustment—A rally or recession in a minor movement. In the first instance, it results from short selling and in the second from taking profits on long trades. Dropping a rubber ball from various heights on a hard floor will serve to illustrate what is meant by this term.

TREND—The direction in which a stock or commodity is moving in a major movement.

UNDERWRITING—A person or company that guarantees the sale of an issue of stocks or bonds.

UNLISTED ISSUES—Issues traded in but not regularly listed on any Exchange. Trading in these is usually "over the counter" transactions. The low-priced ones are usually questionable. (See under STOCKS.)

UNLOADING—Selling at the market, holdings of stocks or commodities.

WASH SALES—Are transactions in which buyer and seller are employed with the object of creating a semblance of activity.

WHEN, AS AND IF ISSUED—Stock or bond transactions made in anticipation of their being issued.

WIPED OUT—A term used in bucket shop transactions, meaning the margin is exhausted.

YIELD—This term is used to indicate the per cent. a stock or bond brings the owner when bought at a stated price, regardless of the regular dividend or interest rate.

ESTABLISHED 1906

This Letter is a Privileged Communication and is Intended for Subscribers ONLY. It must therefore be treated as confidential by the Recipient. Making public the contents thereof shall operate as a forfeiture of my Market Letter Service.

W. C. MOORE'S MARKET LETTER

STOCKS, GRAIN AND COTTON

LOCK BOX 60
WALL STREET STATION

Daily Letter Service $15 per month in advance
Three-Times-a-Week $7.50 per month in advance
Daily Letter Service Including Wire Service $30 per month in advance

52 WALL STREET
NEW YORK.

Always have 20 points reserve behind your trades
PHONE: HANOVER 2399

Prices of Rules

The price of *Rules* 1-2-4-5-7-8-9-10 is $15 each. For the present, one of these Rules will be furnished *FREE* in connection with a monthly subscription for my *Daily Advisory Market Letter Service* or for 2 consecutive months' subscription for the *Tri-Weekly Letters.* The price of *Rule* 3 is $50 and of *Rule* 6 $50. *Rule* 3 goes *FREE* with a *five months' Daily* subscription and *Rule* 6 with a five months' *Daily* subscription. The entire set of *Rules*, together with the *minor Rules* and the *SPECIALS* or *EXTRAS*, with full and explicit *instructions* and *explanations* will be furnished in connection with a year's subscription for my *Daily Market Letters*, for the sum of $150 *payable in advance.*

NOTE. Subscribers for both editions of the *Market Letters* are entitled to *personal letters, personal interviews* and *'phone calls*, relating to market affairs.

Extras

In addition to the Rules above referred to, yearly subscribers will be furnished with *SPECIALS* or *EXTRAS* on the following subjects:

1. **PUTS AND CALLS.**
2. **BUYING AND SELLING MODES.**
3. **THE UNKNOWN AND THE KNOWN IN THEIR PSYCHOLOGICAL RELATION TO MARKET MOVEMENTS.**

Above is a part of a page taken from a booklet entitled: "How to Succeed In Speculation" (Copyright 1917, 1918, 1920 by W. C. Moore). The reader will note the prices charged for the Rules. These Rules are to be found in this work—*amplified.*

INDEX